Research Foundation Year in Review

2012

RESEARCH FOUNDATION

OF CFA INSTITUTE

Statement of Purpose

The Research Foundation of CFA Institute is a not-for-profit organization established to promote the development and dissemination of relevant research for investment practitioners worldwide.

ISBN 978-1-934667-58-3

7 June 2013

Contents

Message from the Chair

As chair of the Research Foundation of CFA Institute's Board of Trustees, I would like to thank you for your interest in and support of the Research Foundation. It is because of you that we are able to advance the understanding of investment markets.

Established in 1965 and endowed by generous contributions from a number of prominent investment professionals and organizations, the Research Foundation of CFA Institute is governed by an all-volunteer board of trustees and supported by a small staff. Our mission is to provide in-depth, high-quality investment research to the global investment community. This worldwide audience reflects the diversity of the modern investment industry—security analysts, portfolio managers, traders, brokers, consultants, fund sponsors (staff as well as trustees), and academics. It includes CFA Institute members and non-members alike.

To address the needs of such a broad audience, Research Foundation authors are practitioners and academics who are committed to producing investment research that is oriented to the practical application of investment finance. The research topics cover all fields relevant to investment professionals, and although that coverage may involve topical investment issues, the Research Foundation's research is meant to distinguish itself not by its timeliness but rather its timelessness.

The majority of our research is published in book form, but we also produce literature reviews, webinars, occasional papers, and seminars on investment issues of particular interest. Notably, the Research Foundation hosts a workshop that is held just prior to the start of the CFA Institute Annual Conference. All Research Foundation materials are distributed online for free, with the hardcopy version offered at a low price.

I hope you enjoy this issue of the *Research Foundation Year in Review.* I urge you to explore the impressive body of research that the Research Foundation has produced over the years. We welcome your comments and suggestions on how best to expand and distribute that work.

Jeffery V. Bailey, CFA
Chair,
Research Foundation of CFA Institute

Executive Director's Report

Welcome to the first issue of the *Research Foundation Year in Review*. The goal of this annual publication is to provide relevant, high-quality investment information in a concise, easy-to-read format. The *Year in Review* summarizes the offerings from the Research Foundation of CFA Institute over the past year—books, literature reviews, workshop presentations, and other relevant material. We are excited about this new publication, and we hope you find the information valuable and useful in enhancing your skills as an investment professional.

Looking Back: 2012

The year 2012 was another exciting year for the Research Foundation. We published four books and two literature reviews on a variety of relevant investment topics (discussed further in the Research Director's Report). In addition, the successful 11th Annual Workshop for the Practitioner was held in Chicago and featured the prominent investment professionals Elroy Dimson and Richard Sandor as speakers and Research Foundation Board of Trustees member Fred Speece, CFA, as moderator. At the workshop, the Vertin Award was given to Elroy Dimson, who joins a distinguished list of past winners, including Bill Sharpe, Marty Leibowitz, and Peter Bernstein.

In 2012, we not only continued to publish high-quality, relevant investment content but also worked hard to develop new ways for you to consume that content. As a result, we introduced book summaries and translated selected summaries so you could gain value from the content with just a modest time commitment. We also created audiobooks to join workshop videos and e-learning sessions on an expanding list of multimedia offerings that can be viewed for free on the website.

CFA Institute societies made important contributions to the scope of operations for the Research Foundation in 2012, with nearly one-third of the 138 societies participating in some form of Research Foundation activity. Many exciting new society programs were introduced by the Research Foundation, including book donations, the Research Foundation author series of speeches, summary translations, book clubs, Research Challenge presentations, and society outreach.

Many of these activities evolved out of the Research Foundation Society Award that was granted for the first time in 2012. We congratulate the award-winning societies from Argentina and Uruguay, Boston, Buffalo, Bulgaria, Rochester, and Seattle for their outstanding efforts using Research Foundation resources as part of their programs and activities. We are looking forward to continuing this tradition of society cooperation in future years.

Just as societies have assisted with carrying out the mission of the Research Foundation, so too have hundreds of volunteers and donors. Their contributions to the Research Foundation since its inception have been instrumental in developing and disseminating our content. A select few of these individuals were chosen for the prestigious Leadership Circle in recognition of their substantial contributions. We were honored to welcome Gary Brinson, CFA, George Noyes, CFA, Wally Stern, CFA, and Jim Vertin, CFA, to the inaugural class of award recipients. In addition to the Leadership Circle, Gary Brinson was further honored by a named research director position, the Gary P. Brinson Director of Research, in recognition of his substantial financial support of the Research Foundation.

Despite all of the positive developments in 2012, the Research Foundation was saddened by the loss of one of our own, John Nagorniak, CFA. As former chairman and longtime board member, John was a tireless worker and inspirational force in guiding the Research Foundation to new heights. He will be missed by us all.

Looking Ahead: 2013

I am proud of our accomplishments in 2012 and look forward to our offerings in 2013. Our pipeline of future content has never looked stronger, and we are positioned to provide you with years of valuable information, including upcoming books on life annuities, derivatives, manager selection, exchange-traded funds, and hedge funds in addition to literature reviews on ethics, asset/liability management, and governance.

It is truly an honor to serve as executive director of the Research Foundation. I would like to thank CFA Institute, the Research Foundation Board of Trustees, and the societies, universities, organizations, volunteers, and donors for making all that we do possible.

Bud Haslett, CFA
Executive Director,
Research Foundation of CFA Institute

Research Director's Report

In 2012, authors selected and, in many cases, financially supported by the Research Foundation of CFA Institute added four books and two literature reviews to the library shelf of investment literature for professionals.

Monographs

Antti Ilmanen, *Expected Returns on Major Asset Classes.* In *Expected Returns on Major Asset Classes* (June 2012), fund manager Antti Ilmanen explores methods of determining the return investors can expect from stocks, government bonds, corporate bonds, and alternative investments. (This last category, in Ilmanen's formulation, consists of real estate, commodity futures, hedge funds, and private equity.) Ilmanen's distinctive approach is to examine each major issue from more than one point of view. The equity risk premium, for example, is considered from the following perspectives:

- Historical—what return have investors earned?
- Forward-looking demand—what return do investors require at this moment in light of current prices?
- Forward-looking supply—what return is reasonable to expect in light of corporate profitability and growth prospects?

Ilmanen uses similarly diverse approaches to examine the various bond risk premiums—long-term bonds over short-term bills and corporates over governments. Alternative investments are likewise studied from multiple angles. The result is a rich intellectual pastiche that challenges readers to think for themselves about their return expectations for each of these basic building blocks of an investment portfolio.

David Tuckett and Richard J. Taffler, *Fund Management: An Emotional Finance Perspective.* A British team consisting of the psychoanalyst David Tuckett and the finance scholar Richard J. Taffler set out to examine how fund managers' emotional responses to stimuli, such as gains or losses on a stock, affect their decision making and investment performance. The result is *Fund Management: An Emotional Finance Perspective* (August 2012). To obtain material for their narrative, the authors interviewed 52 senior fund managers representing 20 institutions in several countries, with special emphasis on a helpful interviewee they call "Duncan Smith," whose emotional life is described in detail. Even for readers familiar with behavioral aspects of finance, the idea of managers "loving" and "hating" stocks or company managements, depending on their contributions to investment performance, will likely be new and different.

Tuckett and Taffler's chief innovation is to portray investment managers' behavior in human terms arising from noninvestment contexts. They note, for example, that managers protect their self-respect and try to retain the respect of others through "storytelling," which they describe as "a wonderfully flexible way of explaining misfortune and managing anxiety without threatening underlying beliefs." This book is an entertaining as well as informative read.

Zvi Bodie, Laurence B. Siegel, and Lisa Stanton, CFA, editors, *Life-Cycle Investing: Financial Education and Consumer Protection.* Over much of the past decade, the Research Foundation has supported a series of conferences at Boston University on the topic of personal investing. The resulting conference proceedings have been published by the Research Foundation, the latest of which is *Life-Cycle Investing: Financial Education and Consumer Protection* (November 2012), edited by Boston University Professor Zvi Bodie, who organizes the conferences; Lisa Stanton, CFA, of the Berkeley, California, office of the asset management firm GMO; and myself. Unlike most conferences, these sessions are explicitly interdisciplinary. They bring together—in addition to the usual finance professors—actuaries, accountants, regulators, news commentators, lawyers, and other habitués of the financial zoo.

The current volume was organized in the aftermath of the 2008 crash. As a result, it focuses on consumer financial protection and other aspects of financial education. Among the many contributors is Nobel Prize–winning economist Robert Merton, who notes that, instead of forcing people to become financial experts in order to be able to save and invest successfully for retirement, we in the profession should just do it for them. No one expects drivers to master the technology behind a car; driving the car is so transparent that a 16-year-old can do it. In the same spirit, investors should be able to "drive" their financial lives with a minimum of technical expertise. Such insights are typical of the contributions to this volume made by the 26 speakers and authors, who in this book focus on lower- and middle-income earners much more than one finds in most of the investment literature.

Momtchil Pojarliev, CFA, and Richard M. Levich, *A New Look at Currency Investing.* In *A New Look at Currency Investing* (December 2012), currency manager Momtchil Pojarliev, CFA, and New York University Professor Richard M. Levich discuss the change in currency investing that has taken place over recent decades. Traditionally, currency management has been a side show, with managers partially or fully hedging currency positions taken for other reasons—say, because a portfolio contains foreign equities and bonds denominated in currencies other than the investor's home currency. The manager may have tried to add alpha, but reducing unintended currency risk was the main reason for the management effort.

Today, currency has become an asset class of its own. Investors may be able to harvest alpha in currency for several reasons. One is that some major players in the currency market—central banks and corporations engaged in international trade—are not mean–variance optimizers and may not even be profit motivated. These conditions leave plenty of space for investors to identify and exploit persistent anomalies.

Pojarliev and Levich begin with a comprehensive description of the foreign exchange, or foreign currency, market. They show how the theorems termed "covered interest parity" and "purchasing power parity" (PPP) can be used for valuation, although according to PPP, currencies drift toward fair value only slowly (on a scale of years or even decades). The authors then present a model in which returns from currency management are separated into alpha and beta components. Finally, they present empirical evidence supporting their model and argue that the relevant benchmark for an active currency manager is not a passive benchmark but a "trading benchmark," such as the Barclay Currency Traders Index, which captures momentum and carry effects.

Literature Reviews

David Adler, "The New Field of Liquidity and Financial Frictions." In "The New Field of Liquidity and Financial Frictions" (June 2012), Barron's reporter and polymath David Adler looks at the "new liquidity movement" in academic finance, which seeks to explain market inefficiencies and macroeconomic dislocations as liquidity events. The new liquidity movement basically argues that the crash of 2007–2009 was one big margin call.

In traditional finance theory, Adler writes, "liquidity plays no role at all because it is assumed away: Markets are frictionless, and participants are price takers." Adler classifies liquidity concerns into those arising from *market illiquidity* and those arising from *funding illiquidity*. Market illiquidity in the real world is caused by fees and spreads, price pressure (meaning that investors are *not* price takers), and inability to trade.

Funding illiquidity comes from practical restrictions on borrowing or selling short. Traditional finance ignores funding illiquidity by assuming you can borrow as much as you want, at the riskless rate, to take long or short positions of any size in any asset. Because a margin call is the withdrawal of funding liquidity, traditional academic finance says there cannot be such a thing as a margin call—or, for that matter, any risk to an investment strategy from position limits, capital requirements, requirements to hold only securities with certain ratings, or borrowing rates higher than the riskless rate.

As everyone knows, however, the real world doesn't work that way—and the crash of 2007–2009 made some financial models look foolish because the models did not allow for the possibility of events unfolding as they did. Academic finance, as a discipline, lost credibility during this period.

The new liquidity theorists, having seen some of the core assumptions of conventional finance overturned, seek to build new analytical tools to study a world in which such events are possible. The literature review identifies the main articles in this exciting new body of literature.

Stephen E. Wilcox, CFA, "Equity Valuation and Inflation: A Review." In "Equity Valuation and Inflation" (January 2012), Minnesota State University (Mankato) Professor Stephen Wilcox, CFA, examines the idea that because stocks are theoretically real assets, they should be neutral to inflation, but in practice, the relationship between unexpected inflation and equity returns has been strongly negative. This review appraises the literature on this question and attempts to reconcile theory with reality.

Most of the literature on equities and inflation comes from the United States in the late 1970s and early 1980s, when the unexpected component of inflation was first very high, then very low (negative). Stock returns in this period were first sharply negative, then very high. The negative correlations from this period dominate the entire history of this discussion because inflation rates have not changed much since that period. Famously, Franco Modigliani and Richard Cohn ("Inflation, Rational Valuation and the Market," *Financial Analysts Journal*, March/April 1979) predicted the 1980s bull market based on a "money illusion" argument. The money illusion approach sharply rejected the efficient market hypothesis and asserted that, at the time, the equity market was discounting real cash flows at nominal discount rates.

As markets have become more global, research on equity returns and inflation has shifted to non-U.S. markets, where changes in inflation in the past two decades have been more substantial. Citing Shu-Chin Lin's 2009 study of 16 countries ("Inflation and Real Stock Return Revisited," *Economic Inquiry*, October 2009), Wilcox notes that "anticipated inflation and inflation uncertainty . . . have negative long-run effects on real stock returns [but] . . . unanticipated inflation . . . [has] a positive short-run effect on real stock returns."

Joint Ventures

The Research Foundation book *Expected Returns on Major Asset Classes* is an adaptation of the core chapters of Antti Ilmanen's longer book titled *Expected Returns: An Investor's Guide to Harvesting Market Rewards*, which John Wiley & Sons published in 2011 in collaboration with the Research Foundation. From time to time, the Research Foundation engages in joint ventures like this one.

Another recent example is M. Barton Waring's *Pension Finance* (2011), also published jointly with Wiley. The Waring book is not paired with a Research Foundation book but, in reflection of the financial and editorial support given to Waring by the Research Foundation, bears the Research Foundation name and the Wiley name on its cover. The book addresses the many difficult issues faced by traditional defined-benefit pension managers in today's environment of low interest rates, poor recent market returns, and limited corporate and public-sector support for such plans. Waring's principal theme can be briefly summarized as follows: If you want your employees to have a defined-benefit pension, you have to fully pay for it instead of relying on market returns to make up for stingy pension contributions.

Summary

We hope that readers find our authors' contributions to the investment literature in 2012 to be at once original, challenging, and practical. We will be publishing a great deal more work of this caliber in coming years.

Laurence B. Siegel
Gary P. Brinson Director of Research,
Research Foundation of CFA Institute

Tribute

Our friend John Nagorniak, CFA, died on 7 September 2012 after a long illness. We at the Research Foundation of CFA Institute are saddened but will always be grateful for his remarkable accomplishments as a trustee from 2004 to 2011 and as our chair from 2008 to 2010. John's history bears testimony to his wide range of skills and his steady hand as chair. He possessed a rare combination of patience and calm through thick and thin. His ability to simplify complex issues and his keen devotion to pushing the frontiers of the Research Foundation's research will resonate forever.

He was a natural leader throughout his career, serving as:

- President and CEO of Franklin Portfolio Associates for more than 20 years
- Senior vice president and chief investment officer at State Street Bank and Trust Company
- Director of investment technology at John Hancock Mutual Life Insurance Company
- President of the Boston Security Analysts Society
- Director of the MIT investment committee
- Treasurer for his Princeton University class on several occasions

John was a graduate of Princeton University and the MIT Sloan School of Management. His array of capabilities, his generosity of time, and his spot-on insights made the businesses and organizations he touched significantly better. Perhaps his strongest contribution was to quantitative investment management in its formative stages. His deep understanding of the math behind groundbreaking discoveries was remarkable. But perhaps more remarkable was John's ability to convey the essence of those discoveries to others. He was a quintessential pioneer, interpreter, and practitioner.

The Research Foundation and CFA Institute community of more than 100,000 members worldwide express their heartfelt appreciation for John Nagorniak's lifetime devotion and their sorrow at losing such a friend. To his family, the Research Foundation expresses our deepest sympathies. We are grateful for the opportunity to have known and worked with such a gentleman.

Expected Returns on Major Asset Classes (a summary)

Antti Ilmanen
Published 2012 by the Research Foundation of CFA Institute
Summary prepared by Antti Ilmanen

Introduction

Expected returns are arguably the most important input into investment decisions. Many investors determine their expectations for returns on investments on the basis of subjective views. More objective predictions are anchored on historical experience, financial theories, and prevailing market conditions.

In my book *Expected Returns: An Investor's Guide to Harvesting Market Rewards* (Chichester, U.K.: John Wiley & Sons, 2011), I tackle this broad topic in a comprehensive manner; this shorter book, in contrast, adapts four of my central chapters on asset class returns (stocks, government bonds, corporate bonds, and alternatives). Both books stress that the traditional paradigm of expected return estimation should be broadened in two ways: (1) moving beyond the narrow perspective of asset class investing to focus additionally on expected returns for active strategy styles and for underlying factors and (2) reducing the focus on historical performance and widening the set of inputs used. Following these principles results in two key benefits: better-diversified portfolios and more forward-looking analysis.

Broadening Away from Equity Concentration and Asset Class Perspective. Even though many investors have improved portfolio diversification by shifting from home-biased holdings to truly global investments and by expanding their asset class opportunity set, they still largely rely on the equity premium for long-term returns. Both 60%/40% stock/bond portfolios and "endowment model" portfolios (which make significant investments in alternatives) have high stock market betas, and equity risk often accounts for 90% of the portfolio risk budgets in either type of portfolio.

This book drills into the building blocks of asset class diversification: the equity premium, term and credit premia in fixed income, and the performance of the main alternative assets (real estate, commodities, hedge funds, and private equity). My 2011 book argues further that by looking *beyond* asset class allocation, investors can achieve more effective portfolio diversification. The book uses a three-dimensional cube to help readers visualize adding to the asset class perspective by including the complementary viewpoints of *strategy styles* and *risk factors*.

- *Strategy styles.* The strategy style perspective is important for understanding the profit potential of popular active trading styles. Empirical research shows that the characteristics of cheap valuations, high starting yields, and recent success (momentum) have provided long-run performance tailwinds in almost any investment context studied, often comparable in magnitude to the equity premium. The relation between volatility and future returns is tenuous and is often negative within an asset class.
- *Underlying factors.* Sophisticated investors are increasingly trying to look beyond asset classes and strategies in order to identify the underlying factors driving their portfolio returns. Each asset can be viewed as a bundle of characteristics or systematic factor exposures that largely determine its expected returns. For example, a corporate bond portfolio is subject to interest rate and default risks. Even more fundamentally, it is exposed to fluctuations in inflation and real rates, to gyrations in global and firm-specific growth, and to liquidity and volatility developments.

In summary, it is helpful to view investment returns from many angles—which asset classes earn them, what active strategy types deliver them, what underlying factors explain them. The broadened perspective helps investors *harvest market rewards from multiple sources to achieve more effective portfolio diversification and superior risk-adjusted returns.*

Balanced Inputs: Less Historical Extrapolation, More Forward-Looking Analysis. Perhaps the most common investor mistake is chasing returns by overweighting stocks, sectors, asset classes, or strategies that have been successful in recent years. In fact, extrapolating past performance *from recent months* can be moderately profitable, as the record of momentum investors shows; sadly, most investors appear to extrapolate *over multi-year windows* when reversal tendencies have taken over.

Judgments about the expected returns of any investment are based on different mixtures of the following four inputs: (1) historical average returns, (2) financial and behavioral theories, (3) forward-looking market indicators (such as yields and valuation ratios), and (4) discretionary views. The challenge is to refine the art of investment decision making in a way that exploits all our knowledge about each of the four inputs without being unduly dependent on any one of them.

Historical Performance. Historical average returns are a common starting point for judging expected returns. If expected returns are constant over time, the long-run average realized return is a good estimate of expected future return. Longer historical windows reduce sample specificity and enable more accurate estimates of average returns, but historical data from the distant past may be irrelevant because of structural changes and may have much lower quality than recent data. Even worse, any cyclical variation in expected returns over time makes extrapolation of multi-year performance particularly dangerous. Periods of high realized returns and rising asset valuations—think stock markets in the 1990s—are often associated with falling forward-looking returns. Finally, various selection biases can overstate published returns. These concerns notwithstanding, we should learn from history while being wary of excessive extrapolation and hindsight biases.

Theory. The state of finance theory has changed dramatically over the past 30 years, away from the restrictive theories of the single-factor capital asset pricing model, efficient markets, and constant expected returns. Current academic views are more diverse, less tidy, and more realistic. Expected returns are now commonly seen as driven by multiple factors. Some determinants are rational (risk and liquidity premia); others, irrational (biases such as extrapolation and overconfidence). The expected return on any investment may vary over time, again for rational or irrational reasons.

A central insight from finance theories that start with the assumption of investor rationality is that required investment returns have little to do with an investment's stand-alone volatility and more to do with the co-variation of its losses with "bad times." Investors should require high-risk premia for assets that tend to fare poorly in bad times (think of recessions, equity bear markets, and financial crises—or their combination in 2008). In contrast, safe-haven assets (such as government bonds since at least the late 1990s) can justify low or even negative risk premia.

Forward-Looking Analysis. Forward-looking indicators, such as valuation ratios, have a better track record in forecasting asset class returns than do rearview-mirror measures. The practice of using the historical average return as the best estimate of future return—as is often done with the equity premium—relies on the idea of constant expected returns. The boom–bust cycles of the past decade have helped to cause both academic and practitioner views to shift toward accepting the idea of time-varying expected returns. As a result, institutional investors no longer reject market timing out of hand.

While I endorse some amount of market timing based on tactical market forecasts, it is important to stress humility. Hindsight bias makes us forget how difficult forecasting is, especially in highly competitive financial markets. Expected returns are unobservable, and our understanding of them is limited. Even the best experts' forecasts are noisy estimates of prospective returns.

Equity Risk Premium

Historical annual excess returns of U.S. stocks over government bonds average 3% to 5% over long data windows, a further 1% over short-dated bills, and about another 2% higher if arithmetic means are used. Global excess returns of stocks over bonds are somewhat lower.

Forward-looking measures of the equity–bond premium exhibit significant time variation, probably for both rational and irrational reasons. The dividend discount model states that long-run real equity returns equal the sum of the dividend yield and the real dividend growth rate (assuming no valuation changes), currently adding up to 3% to 4%.

Both yield and growth inputs can be debated, but estimates in the past decade point to modest real returns. Any higher expected return estimates must be justified by using broader payout yields, more optimistic growth inputs, or expanding valuation multiples. However, the real long-run growth rates of dividends and earnings per share have clearly lagged the GDP growth rate. In addition, equity market valuations have been low when inflation is high or when there is deflation; valuations have been higher when inflation is low and positive.

Valuation, cyclical, and sentiment indicators can be useful for market timing, but all such relations are fragile.

Bond Risk Premium

The bond risk premium (BRP), or term premium, is the expected return advantage of long-duration government bonds over short-term (one-period) bonds. Historical average U.S. Treasury returns increase with duration, especially at short durations. The realized average excess return is about 1% but is higher during periods when falling yields give unexpected windfall gains.

The yield curve reflects both the BRP and the market's interest rate expectations. Yield curve steepness is a noisy measure of either part. Since rate expectations taint the information about the BRP in the yield curve, a natural solution is to estimate the rate expectations—for example, with the help of survey data—and subtract them from bond yields.

The survey-based BRP has been driven primarily by a level-dependent inflation premium—rising in the 1960s and 1970s from near zero to 3% or 4% and then falling back in the 1980s and 1990s. Other key drivers of the

BRP are safe-haven, supply/demand, and cyclical factors. Since the late 1990s, Treasuries' valuable safe-haven role has contributed to a negative BRP.

Duration timing models predict near-term bond returns. A steep yield curve, weak economic growth, and weak equity markets, as well as positive bond market momentum, have historically been bullish indicators.

Credit Risk Premium

Bonds exposed to credit risk have outperformed Treasuries only marginally over long histories (by 0.2% to 0.5% annually for investment-grade credits), arguably giving poor compensation for their lower liquidity and bad timing of losses. Long-dated corporate bonds have performed especially poorly, while barely speculative-grade bonds (BB rated) and short-dated top-rated credits have offered pockets of long-run value.

Credit spreads are observable measures of the prospective return advantage of risky assets over "riskless" Treasuries. However, spreads overstate this advantage because they do not include a decrement for expected losses from default or downgrading, embedded options, or damaging trading activity (such as selling BB-rated "fallen angels").

Spread variation over time reflects the scarcity and liquidity edge of Treasuries over other issues as well as cyclical, volatility, and default developments. Credit spreads have some ability to predict excess returns, as do various cyclical and supply/demand indicators.

Alternative Asset Premia

The last chapter covers the main alternative asset classes: real estate, commodities, hedge funds, and private equity. The first two are real assets added to traditional portfolios more for their diversification and inflation-hedging properties, while the last two are active funds often brought in more as return enhancers.

Common characteristics of alternatives include lower liquidity than traditional assets, an intended role as diversifiers (but often high correlation with equity markets), and growing popularity in the past decade. Long-run returns for alternatives may reflect a combination of traditional and alternative risk premia, including compensation for illiquidity. Because these drivers differ for the four alternatives, I discuss each of them separately.

Real estate can be accessed directly through less liquid physical markets or indirectly through listed REITs and property stocks. The long-run return of real estate is between that of bonds and stocks, but starting valuations matter. Long-run real price growth is modest, but rental yield income can be large.

Commodity futures are perhaps the best diversifiers of financial assets and are also the best inflation hedges. Long-run average returns reflect both futures' roll returns and spot price appreciation. Oil-related futures have given the highest returns as well as the best diversification and hedging properties.

Hedge fund index data suggest that these funds have been able to add value, even as a group and after fees, unlike traditional managers. Critics question how much the documented outperformance reflects biases in reported fund returns or various risks (traditional and alternative betas, illiquidity, tail risks). I review attempts to quantify these biases and risks.

Private equity funds have a less impressive track record as a group than other alternatives, according to academic studies. Adjusting for reporting biases and some risks, they do not outperform listed equities, despite their liquidity disadvantage. To outperform after fees, investors need to be able to pick top-quartile managers.

* * * * * *

The complete monograph can be found at http://www.cfapubs.org/doi/abs/10.2470/rf.v2012.n1.1.

Use your smartphone to scan the QR code to go straight to the webpage.

Fund Management: An Emotional Finance Perspective (a summary)

David Tuckett and Richard J. Taffler
Published 2012 by the Research Foundation of CFA Institute
Summary prepared by David Tuckett and Richard J. Taffler

This book sets out to describe the emotional world of the fund manager. Based on more than 50 in-depth interviews with senior fund managers in the world's largest financial centres managing almost US$10 billion in assets, on average, the research asked the following questions: What is it really like being a money manager? How do money managers make sense of the highly pressurised and demanding environment in which they have to operate? How do they deal with the challenges they have to confront? And what role do their emotions play?

Conventional finance theory typically focuses on the performance of investment professionals and pays little attention to their day-to-day experiences. This important gap in our understanding of the nature of the investment process has major implications for the way financial markets work. By exploring the feelings, emotions, and experiences of real-world asset managers through interviews, we were able to construct a coherent theory of real fund management activity. The report of the findings should also help readers of the book learn from the experiences of their peers.

Emotional finance complements conventional behavioural finance, which explores the impact of cognitive biases on our investment decisions. Emotional finance formally recognises the key role our feelings and emotions, both conscious and, importantly, unconscious, play in the investment process.

Our respondents made clear that feelings and emotions play a key role in the investment task. Rather than viewing emotion as a threat to investment performance, as is often wrongly done, we show how a true understanding of the underlying emotions that drive fund manager behaviour, whether consciously acknowledged or not, is a vital component of effective decision making.

From the interviews, we could draw five main themes that are central to an understanding of the fund manager's task.

First, money managers are required to be exceptional, to outperform on a consistent basis in competition with other equally able and well-resourced fund managers. This expectation inevitably leads to emotional stress.

Second, money managers need to make decisions on the basis of a mass of incomplete, and often unreliable or conflicting, information. Investment judgements, therefore, are inevitably based on interpreting information that is inherently ambiguous in nature, which again has emotional ramifications.

Third, asset managers believe that, although market prices can diverge from fundamental value in the short term, prices converge to fundamental value in the longer term. However, because no one knows how long the convergence will take, investment decision making is based on predicting a future that is inherently uncertain.

Fourth, to be effective, fund managers believe they need to have an information advantage. They cannot know, however, whether they have an advantage or whether others are able to interpret the same information set better than they can. This ambiguity, again, leads to anxiety.

Finally, and most importantly, our interviews made clear that the relationships fund managers have with their stocks are highly emotional in nature. Even though many of our respondents claimed their competitive advantage was their ability to be emotion free, they often got carried away when talking about the stocks. They revealed that they liked and even loved stocks and managements of companies that were delivering what the mangers were hoping for and then hated the companies when they let the money managers down. Fund management is a process in which asset managers become excited in anticipation of desired future outcomes and then disappointed when things don't work out. Fund managers' feelings about their stocks are strong and volatile.

We believe that these five dimensions of the asset management task are experienced by any investment professional. In our book, we illustrate how these themes may combine and create feelings of emotional conflict and how coping with these situations is at the heart of what investment professionals have to do.

We believe that professional money managers will find that what we report from our interviews resonates with their own experiences and reveals the practical issues they face in decision making. Importantly, drawing on the insights of emotional finance, we provide a language that allows readers to talk about their own experiences and to understand the pressures under which they have to operate.

Lessons that can be learnt from this book include the recognition that all fund managers' relationships with their investments generate emotional ambivalence. This finding has implications for, for example, how to deal with buying, selling, and holding stocks when the market is going against them. We illustrate the lesson that stress and the continuous pressure by clients (and often by employers) to perform both in the short term and the long term, irrespective of the stated mandate, are dysfunctional and not conducive to reflective analysis. We describe some of the practical ways our respondents deal with the conflicting demands placed on them and their associated high levels of anxiety. One of the clear findings is the key role a facilitative managerial environment can play in helping asset managers do their job effectively.

One of the most interesting findings of our research is how fund managers generate the conviction to act, keep their nerve, and deal with stocks that underperform by using investment 'narratives' or telling stories in various ways. The stories allow the fund managers to believe that future outcomes are predictable, leading to the commitment to act. Interestingly our quantitative managers used stories in exactly the same way as their more traditional stock-picking colleagues.

We discuss how the characteristics of the *real* risks money managers experience and are concerned about are very different from conventional statistical measures of risk used in the finance literature. The real risks to their performance generates strong emotions that are not generally recognised. Becoming aware of such feelings can help fund managers deal with the uncertainty and lack of predictability about future outcomes that they continually face. We show how the money managers we interviewed deal with real risk in their investments and portfolios.

The final chapter of the book draws on the insights of emotional finance to help us understand the characteristics of the fund manager's task. We demonstrate that the conventional distinction between rational and irrational behaviour is not meaningful and should be abandoned. All investment decision making involves emotion and intuition. Avoiding acknowledging these realities leads to a repressed state of mind.

Building on this insight, we point out how characterising investment as being about 'greed, fear, and hope', as is done conventionally, is wrong. Based on the experiences of the fund managers we interviewed, what really characterises money management is 'excitement, anxiety, and denial'. Not recognising this distinction can only lead to even more dysfunctional investment processes.

Fund management is invariably a highly emotional activity. It is driven not by conscious feelings alone but also by unconscious drives of which we are not directly aware. These feelings and drives are highly influential in determining investment behaviour. This emotional context has major implications for the nature of the asset management industry and the basis on which it operates. We conclude by arguing that an understanding of this context can lead to a more realistic view of the role of the fund manager, better comprehension of the asset management industry generally, and an appreciation of money management's real contribution in enhancing client welfare.

* * * * * *

The complete monograph can be found at http://www.cfapubs.org/doi/abs/10.2470/rf.v2012.n2.1.

Use your smartphone to scan the QR code to go straight to the webpage.

Life-Cycle Investing: Financial Education and Consumer Protection (a summary)

Edited by Zvi Bodie, Laurence B. Siegel, and Lisa Stanton, CFA
Published 2012 by the Research Foundation of CFA Institute
Summary prepared by Laurence B. Siegel

The third conference on the future of life-cycle saving and investing, entitled "Financial Education and Consumer Financial Protection," was held at the Boston University School of Management on 23–25 May 2011. Like the previous two conferences, it was organized by Professor Zvi Bodie of Boston University and financially supported by the Research Foundation of CFA Institute, the Federal Reserve Bank of Boston, and Boston University. Also as in the previous conferences, speakers from a wide variety of disciplines, not just finance, offered their perspectives.

Keynote Speaker: Robert Merton

The Nobel Prize–winning economist Robert Merton was the keynote speaker. He asked whether financial innovation and engineering would be helpful in keeping financial decision-making simple for the ordinary person. He addressed this question through the lens of a product he has been working on—namely, a retirement income solution for retirement-provided plans. He began by defining the goal as a given level of income rather than wealth—having 10,000 pounds a year, as Jane Austen's fictitious (and wealthy) Mr. Darcy is described, rather than 200,000 pounds of net worth. The desire for simplicity means that the product has to work by itself, he explained, without a financial planner or other expert.

The risk-free asset is then identified as a deferred annuity (like a traditional pension payout) instead of cash, which is considered to be the riskless asset in most analyses. Unfortunately, deferred annuities are subject to a number of regulatory and practical hurdles and to credit risk. But the ideal portfolio for a would-be retiree is some combination of deferred annuities, representing risk-free investing, and a world market portfolio of equities, capturing the payoff for taking risk.

Merton concluded by recommending that we not force advanced financial education on surgeons, truck drivers, and others disinclined to learn about investing. Instead, we should make the technology transparent, in the same way that automotive engineers have made automobile technology almost invisible to the user, who, for example, can drive a modern car using the same skills he or she acquired in 1955 when first learning to drive. "We can make smart consumers. . . ," said Merton, "by creating products that make them smart rather than by literally educating them. Intelligent product design and oversight can be an effective substitute for consumer financial education" (p. 13).

Opening Remarks: Elizabeth Duke

Elizabeth Duke is a member of the board of governors of the Federal Reserve System. She began by summarizing recent economic and investment trends, including tendencies to save too little, retire early, use retirement savings for nonretirement purposes, and (only recently) rent instead of buying a house. She then made recommendations for financial education: Start early ("math problems [in school] can involve consumer financial calculations"), take advantage of "teachable" moments, and think imaginatively about the use of social media and new technologies (p. 24). Duke concluded with highlights from Doorways to Dreams and other youth financial education programs, including finance-related games, and noted that finance education is most effective when it can be tied to actual life outcomes.

Session 1: Consumer Finance 101 for Financial Educators, Financial Advisers, and Regulators

Bodie moderated a panel composed of Stephen Horan of CFA Institute, John Gannon of the FINRA Investor Education Foundation,[1] Peter Tufano of the University of Oxford, and Chris Farrell of the public radio program *Marketplace Money*.

Horan emphasized three ideas: (1) the need for humility in investor education because we don't know much about its efficacy; (2) the need to define the goals of education and think about what behavior we are trying to motivate; and (3) the need to emphasize numeracy, the ability to use numbers. He drew an extensive analogy between investor education and driver education. In both, there are three skill levels: (1) "the skills that everybody needs to have," (2) "an intermediate set of skills for those who. . . reasonably choose to take on more-advanced tasks," and (3) "some highly advanced skills that really ought to be left to the experts." In investing, the first set includes budgeting and debt management; the second set includes "compounding, dollar cost averaging, and diversification," and the third set includes "risk management, asset allocation, and security selection" (p. 30).

Gannon focused on financial fraud. He noted that the typical fraud victim fits a surprising profile: "male, 55–65 years of age, married, more financially literate, college educated, recently subjected to a change in financial or health

[1]FINRA is the Financial Industry Regulatory Authority, the industry self-regulating entity in the United States.

status, a risk taker, self-directed, and overly optimistic" (p. 34). While such investors may not be the most susceptible to fraud, they are overrepresented simply because they have more investments, and more complex investments, than most people. Frauds usually have a number of psychosocial factors in common: the promise of great riches, apparent credibility of the source, social consensus (other people participating in the fraudulent investment), reciprocity (thinking that one owes something to the fraudster), and scarcity (thinking that the fraudulent investment is hard to get). Gannon concluded by offering suggestions for fraud avoidance.

Tufano began by noting that the knowledge base of most investors is very poor but their self-regard is not: They often believe themselves to be knowledgeable. He then discussed whether financial institutions might be providing good service as a substitute for having informed customers and suggested that the answer is no. For example, broker-sold mutual funds perform worse than directly sold funds, even before adjusting for the difference in fees, which are higher for broker-sold funds. Likewise, banks take advantage of consumers by charging foolish customers (e.g., those who overdraw their accounts often) high fees that are then used to subsidize wise customers (who never overdraw). Tufano recommended that more effort go into the "architecture for making choices," intended to nudge consumers toward better decisions, and into "encourag[ing] financial institutions to deliver better products and services and hold[ing] them to higher fiduciary duties" (p. 40). He concluded with an "outrageous suggestion: We hijack not only the SAT exam but also the PSAT and ACT exams." Students, he argued, do not care if the exam tests "whether two trains are coming closer together or whether the balances on a savings and an investment account are getting further apart" (p. 42). If the latter is taught, financial education can be achieved through the back door of preparation for standardized testing.

Farrell noted that most of the callers on his radio show ask about student loans and retirement savings. He also noted that the poor can benefit the most from financial education because "being poor. . . costs a lot of money" (p. 43). Farrell discussed the barrier to college education due to FAFSA (the complex student loan application), as well as favorable outcomes when financial literacy requirements are tied to certain types of aid to individuals. He concluded with a number of useful suggestions for getting people to save more.

Session 2: Housing Decisions: Do Consumers Know What They Need to Know?

Paul Willen of the Federal Reserve Bank of Boston made a presentation entitled "Disclosure in the Mortgage Market," which was then discussed by the Wellesley College professor Karl Case, Christopher Mayer of the Columbia Business School, and Robert Lerman of the Urban Institute and American University.

Willen focused on the Consumer Financial Protection Bureau's (CFPB's) proposed disclosure to borrowers who are getting a mortgage. The idea behind the proposed disclosure is that borrowers need a simple, clear explanation of the important parts of their mortgage. At the top of the proposed form (shown by the speaker) are the key loan terms, which show the interest rate and how it could change, the monthly payment and how it could change, and the taxes and insurance and how they could change. Much of the rest of the form continues to focus on how payments could change, reflecting the prevailing view that the mortgage crisis was due to increases in required mortgage payments.

But Willen argued that the crisis was caused instead by falling house prices, so the proposed disclosure wouldn't do much good. "Some people think that a lot of borrowers got into trouble, which pushed house prices down, but that is not what happened," Willen said. "We have had episodes of high delinquency before, but delinquencies do not turn into foreclosures unless house prices are falling" (p. 56). The reason is that if mortgages are not "underwater"—that is, with a mortgage balance higher than the house value—a buyer who gets in trouble can sell the house without needing to pay the loss in cash at the closing and avoid foreclosure.

Willen then proposed an alternative disclosure form that discusses the risk that house prices will fall and the risk that a foreclosure will take place given the terms of the loan, the income of the borrower, and so forth.

In a comment, Karl Case noted that the high interest rate environment of 1979–1981 caused Vancouver house prices to crash but not California house prices. The difference was that fixed-rate mortgages were prevalent in the United States but five-year adjustable mortgages were used in Canada. The adjustable feature destabilized the Canadian housing market.

Mayer said that mortgage prepayment penalties, which are generally poorly regarded and have mostly been abandoned, may be helpful because they

> promote a kind of risk sharing. Consider a pool of borrowers who all take out loans. All the loans represent a similar level of risk, but some of the borrowers end up doing well while others fare poorly. If the borrowers who do well are allowed to pay off their mortgages and drop out of the loan pool, the only people left in the pool are those who have done poorly. (The situation

> is similar to health insurance. If healthy people are allowed to opt out of the insurance pool, the only people left are sick people, who then have to be charged higher premiums.)
>
> Thus, prepayment penalties discourage borrowers from leaving the pool and encourage more viable risk sharing among borrowers. . . . Many other countries have mortgages that are not prepayable, and they have not seen the same level of housing troubles that we have. (p. 63)

Lerman commented on housing from the perspective of the low-income household. He began by noting that many low-income households spend a very high proportion of their income on rent when they could do better by buying. Moreover, low-income housing is surprisingly cheap to buy. He described a hypothetical homeownership voucher program patterned on the Section 8 rent voucher program and suggested a recoupment plan, by which the government can share in capital gains experienced by the subsidized low-income buyer. Lerman enumerated a long list of problems that would be remedied by such a plan.

Session 3: Credit Decisions: Do Consumers Know What They Need to Know?

Mel Stiller, president of Money Management International of Massachusetts, a nonprofit credit counseling agency, made a presentation, upon which William Samuelson of the Boston University School of Management commented.

Stiller began by noting that a legitimate credit counseling agency has three functions: education, counseling, and debt management. In competition with these legitimate agencies are "credit clinics," which offer to repair clients credit for a fee; debt settlement companies, which negotiate with lenders to reduce the principal owed; and agencies that charge the creditor for setting up and administering debt management programs (creditors will pay because they are getting something instead of nothing).

Stiller set forth a list of questions that the Federal Trade Commission says should be asked by consumers seeking credit counseling and debt management. Among them are

- "Does the organization offer a range of services rather than just debt management plans?"
- "Will the agency help develop a plan not just to solve the immediate problem but also to avoid future problems?"
- "What are the fees? Will fees be waived or reduced if they are not affordable?"

- "Are commissions paid to counselors if a debt management plan is established?"
- "Will options other than a [debt management plan] be discussed?" (p. 81)

Stiller concluded with suggestions for better regulatory oversight of the credit counseling business.

Session 4: Saving and Investing by Low- and Middle-Income Households

Lerman and Eugene Steuerle of the Urban Institute presented "The Two Worlds of Personal Finance: Implications for Promoting the Economic Well-Being of Low- and Moderate-Income Families." Moshe Milevsky of York University in Toronto was the discussant, and Laurence Kotlikoff of Boston University moderated.

Conventional personal finance is aimed at investors with liquid assets, generally meaning the well-to-do. But a different kind of personal finance can help people of ordinary means. It is concerned with budgeting, maintaining good credit, and making sensible purchasing and borrowing decisions. Those who want to help people in these circumstances need to keep in mind that most people's largest asset by far is human capital (the discounted present value of future wages) and that Social Security makes up a large fraction of their financial assets. Lerman estimated that the lifetime value of Social Security and Medicare, plus an allowance for public support of nursing-home care, adds to almost $1 million per couple—more, he said, than the private wealth of 75–80% of the population.

Because of the high value of human capital, the most important decision that low- and middle-income people make is when to retire. Each additional year worked increases the post-retirement standard of living by 8% (real). "If they work eight additional years, shifting their retirement age from 62 to 70," Lerman said, "they can typically increase their retirement income by two-thirds or more, which is a lot more than they can obtain through any other portfolio decision" (p. 93).

Poor people rely to a large extent on very high-interest loans, including payday loans and tax refund anticipation loans. The "banked"—those with bank accounts and access to credit through banks or credit unions—do much better than those without these services. It is vitally important to maintain a good credit score.

Lerman concluded that Social Security benefits, homeownership, and pensions are the best ways for low- and middle-income households to have a successful retirement. Social Security benefits depend on a "stable employment record." Houses eventually get paid off, providing free rent to the owner. And employment choices should take the availability of pension plans into account.

Milevsky discussed the book *Portfolios of the Poor.*[2] The book suggests, according to Milevsky, that "low-income people are actually extremely sophisticated in their management of personal finances" (p. 97). The authors of the book interviewed participants selected from among the world's poorest people, and according to the *Economist*,[3] "the subjects used a combination of loans and savings to ensure that their lives were not, literally, hostage to fortune. Hardly anyone lived utterly hand to mouth." On good days, they saved a little money to help them through the anticipated bad days. Milevsky concluded that "economists can learn a lot about consumption smoothing from low- and middle-income households" (p. 98).

Although human capital is the most important asset for most people, it is difficult to convince many people of that fact. For example, accountants say that capitalizing future wages is improper and young people often don't understand the calculation. But when an older audience is asked how much of their financial capital they would give up to be 25 years old again and have their human capital back, they say that they would give up most or all of it. Milevsky concluded that "at some point in our lives, we realize how valuable human capital is. . . . So [we should] put a number on it and start treating it like an asset class" (p. 99).

Session 5: Financial Education: What Have We Learned So Far?

Lewis Mandell of the Aspen Institute Initiative on Financial Security presented a paper entitled "School-Based Financial Education: Not Ready for Prime Time," and Lauren Willis of the Loyola Law School Los Angeles presented "Financial Education: Lessons Not Learned and Lessons Learned."

Mandell compared the effectiveness of financial education with that of sex education based on research findings. In one study he discusses, "educational interventions designed to reduce unwanted pregnancies among adolescents neither delayed initiation of sexual intercourse nor reduced pregnancy rates" (p. 112). Likewise, financial education in high school does not typically help young adults save money, avoid become indebted, or avoid bouncing checks. He said that some types of financial education have been shown to be more effective than others. A short financial or consumer education course has the least favorable outcomes in the research; an economics course has better outcomes; and a stock market game has the best outcomes.

---

[2]Daryl Collins, Jonathan Morduch, Stuart Rutherford, and Orlanda Ruthven. *Portfolios of the Poor: How the World's Poor Live on $2 a Day* (Princeton, NJ: Princeton University Press 2009).
[3]"Smooth Operators," *Economist* (16 May 2009):82 (http://www.economist.com/node/13665319).

Adults fare somewhat better. "Retirement seminars have a positive wealth effect on participation in retirement plans, but . . . participants in retirement seminars had much better intentions than follow-through capabilities"; the dollar amounts of post-seminar increases in contributions to retirement plans are negligible. "Credit counseling tended to improve both borrowing behavior and creditworthiness," and "pre-purchase counseling programs for prospective homebuyers decreased delinquency rates." Mandell concluded that "financial education is most useful if it is specific to important, imminent decisions because pre-purchase motivation to learn is very high" (p. 114). Mandell finished with an extensive set of suggestions for improving financial education and training, including the use of "'plain vanilla' products [that] could be created, vetted, and blessed for each major financial product category for consumers who are not capable of making more complex financial choices" (p. 118).

Willis argued that financial literacy education is unhelpful and should not be pursued. Many studies have shown that consumers who participate in financial education make worse financial decisions than other consumers. This finding applies broadly—to soldiers, bankrupt individuals, high school students, and other populations for whom data could be gathered. One possible reason is that "a little knowledge is a dangerous thing," giving its possessor a false sense of expertise (p. 130). Another is that financial education is often provided at a level of language complexity that most readers cannot comprehend. Finally, financial innovation proceeds more quickly than financial educators can keep up with, so consumers are continually being asked to evaluate products of which they have little or no knowledge.

Attention, according to Willis, should be placed instead on teaching basic math skills: "We might then replace current financial education programs with programs to teach consumers when they need expert help, how to locate competent and trustworthy advisers, and how to implement adviser instructions" (p. 133).

Session 6: Consumer Financial Protection and the Way Forward

Joseph Cherian and Wee Kang Chua, both of the National University of Singapore, and Bodie presented their paper entitled "Worry-Free Inflation-Indexing for Sovereigns: How Governments Can Effectively Deliver Inflation-Indexed Returns to Their Citizens and Retirees."

The authors argued that the availability of assets with payoffs indexed to inflation is key to retirement security. Such assets exist in the United States, the United Kingdom, and some other countries, but most Asian countries do not have them. While anyone can issue inflation-indexed bonds, "government is the natural institution to provide [safe] inflation-linked benefits," the authors said, "because tax revenues (both income and sales taxes) are indexed automatically to inflation" (p. 140).

Investors, according to the authors, are concerned with (1) receiving an adequate level of income every month that (2) is indexed to their cost of living and (3) lasts for as long as they live. Point 1 is dependent on the amount saved or provided in a social benefit, and Point 2 is covered by the existence of inflation-indexed bonds. But Point 3 requires the availability of life annuities. Singapore has begun issuing life annuities, although they are not inflation-indexed. The authors suggested that the simplest way to ensure an inflation-indexed post-retirement income is to build a laddered portfolio of inflation-linked government bonds, with the last bond maturing at the "expected mortality date." This solution, however, does not provide the longevity insurance (income beyond the expected mortality date) that an annuity would provide.

The authors offered technical suggestions on how the governments of smaller countries can "manufacture" inflation-adjusted returns. One way is simply to take on the risk of issuance (the main risk being that the increased payout to investors will not be completely covered by increased tax receipts). Another way is to take positions in the derivatives market, and a third way is to invest in the inflation-indexed bonds of other sovereigns.

* * * * * *

The complete monograph can be found at http://www.cfapubs.org/doi/abs/10.2470/rf.v2012.n3.full.

Use your smartphone to scan the QR code to go straight to the webpage.

A New Look at Currency Investing (a summary)

Momtchil Pojarliev, CFA, and Richard M. Levich
Published 2012 by the Research Foundation of CFA Institute
Summary prepared by Momtchil Pojarliev, CFA, and Richard M. Levich

Currency investing has a fairly short history as a segment of investment management. For most of the 20th century, until the breakup of the Bretton–Woods system in the early 1970s, currency transactions were almost exclusively the province of specialized interbank currency traders and a few sophisticated private and institutional investors. Currency was viewed primarily as a medium of exchange to facilitate international trade and financial transactions, not as an asset in its own right that could be held with the expectation of profit.

The development of currency into a separate investing segment (or asset class) has been gradual but persistent. Through the 1980s, most investment managers acquired currency exposure primarily as a by-product of investing in foreign currency–denominated stocks or bonds. To limit, or hedge, unavoidable currency exposure, managers developed so-called *currency overlay* strategies for actively offsetting risk. But the realization that the currency component of an international portfolio might be actively hedged, and profitably so, led some managers to consider offering currency management as a separate product. With the relaxation of capital controls in many markets, increased capital mobility, and deepening international capital markets, the view that currency is an investable asset has grown.

In *A New Look at Currency Investing*, Momtchil Pojarliev and Richard M. Levich examine the rationale supporting the case for currency investing and present empirical evidence on the most prominent current styles of currency investing. A number of factors—some historical, some institutional, and others grounded in economic theory and policy making—have resulted in currency investing being viewed differently from equity or bond investing. The history of currency investing and market experiences with fluctuating exchange rates are relatively brief compared with these elements for equities and bonds. Moreover, the number of freely floating currencies is limited and some emerging market currencies are subject to limited capital mobility and the possibility of capital controls which raises questions about the diversification potential within an FX-only portfolio. Currency values are notoriously difficult to model, more so than equities, so valuation can be elusive. Currencies are prone to central bank intervention and may be used as instruments of political and/or economic policy. These aspects, coupled with the fact that currency trades in its own market with its own institutions for clearing and settlement, explain why currency has earned a reputation in some quarters as being a highly specialized area for currency professionals only. As a result, many institutional investors have avoided making a role for currency in their portfolios.

There are two basic types of currency mandates. With a currency overlay mandate, the investor already owns a portfolio of foreign debt or equity and the objective is either to entirely eliminate currency risk from the portfolio or partially reduce currency risk while opportunistically going after return. In an absolute return mandate, the investor seeks to earn a positive return, usually in excess of some benchmark and subject to acceptable risk levels.

Pojarliev and Levich focus primarily on the second type and highlight several features of currency returns that make currency an attractive asset class for institutional investors. First, several established currency trading strategies (variants of *carry*, *trend-following*, and *value* strategies) have produced consistent returns that can be proxied as style or risk factors and have the nature of beta returns. The returns to these strategies tend to be imperfectly correlated with traditional equity market returns; thus, they provide a beta benchmark for currency against which returns from more active or idiosyncratic styles of currency management can be compared. Second, Pojarliev and Levich's empirical evidence shows that some currency managers produce true alpha—that is, a positive residual return after the effects of beta-like factors have been removed—even relative to a more demanding expected return benchmark. The potential to earn alpha-like returns as well as beta-like returns heightens the appeal of the currency asset class. Finally, the global currency market offers enormous liquidity, and it continued to function uninterrupted throughout the depths of the 2007–08 global financial crisis. Although certain currency strategies fared poorly during the crisis (in particular, when trades in those strategies were "crowded"), the volume of activity continued to be strong, which allowed nimble players to navigate the market.

The authors provide a thorough description of the structure of the foreign exchange (FX) market as well as the nature of currency management mandates in recent years, and the principal currency investment strategies in wide use. With the advent of floating exchange rates in the early 1970s, many economists theorized that currency prices would take on characteristics similar to other asset prices. Specifically, the notion that short-term currency movements would be random had some empirical support. Yet, many market professionals persisted in the belief (which now has empirical backing) that exchange rates have predictable patterns that allow a technical trading style of currency investing. And exchange rates, like other assets, can be linked to a group of economic fundamentals. The theoretical notions that short-run exchange rate changes are linked to the interest rate differential between foreign and domestic currency deposits (i.e., the concept of uncovered interest parity) and that long-run exchange rates are anchored by relative foreign and domestic price levels (i.e., the concept of purchasing power parity) are common features of nearly all fundamental currency models. Many economic studies provide evidence, however, that both parity conditions have frequent and sometimes persistent violations that are, to some extent, predictable. As a result, exchange rates may be prone to misalignment, which provides underpinning for the adoption of the carry and value-oriented styles of currency investing.

In the past, in virtually all asset classes except currency, research has been able to demonstrate a separation between the alpha and beta components of returns. Pojarliev and Levich propose using style or risk factors to model currency returns in a manner analogous to the application of such factors in other investment contexts. This approach offers a natural way to decompose returns into alpha and beta components in currency management, which allows the authors to investigate the drivers of returns from currency speculation and whether currency managers demonstrate an ability to generate positive alpha. The authors' empirical evidence documents that style factors explain a significant part of the variability of the returns of professional currency managers. Managers may be classified as beta grazers, whose returns can be tightly linked to risk factors, or alpha hunters, who exhibit no significant exposure to the risk factors. The empirical analysis indicates, first, that only alpha hunters have delivered persistent performance regardless of the market environment (low beta or high beta). In periods when the common strategies deliver low or negative returns, a beta grazer cannot be expected to perform well. Second, beta grazers harbor important limitations when the goal is to diversify global equity exposure. For example, the average correlation of the carry strategy with global equities beta is 0 over the long run but approaches 1 in periods of equity crashes. Third, because beta exposure can usually be obtained cheaply thought ETFs, investors should avoid paying alpha fees to beta grazers.

The authors use two datasets of returns of actual currency hedge funds operated by professional managers to investigate a variety of questions: (1) Do currency managers generate alpha? (2) Is past performance any indication of future performance (i.e., are alphas persistent)? (3) Are investment styles (beta exposures) persistent? (4) Is currency investing useful to investors with substantial equity exposure?

The most important results and implications of these analyses are as follows. A substantial proportion of returns earned by active currency managers can be explained by indices of three common currency strategies (carry, trend, and value) and a fourth factor that proxies for volatility in currency markets. As a group, currency managers do not generate alpha returns, a result consistent with empirical evidence in other asset classes. However, a significant minority of managers are able to add positive alpha for their clients. Furthermore, there is evidence of alpha and beta persistence. Past performance data can be an indication of future managerial style and performance for individual managers. Adding even a relatively small allocation of currency exposure to institutional investors' portfolio can make a meaningful positive impact on the portfolio's overall performance characteristics. Not surprisingly, adding currency managers that are alpha generators has a larger impact than adding currency managers that are only generating beta returns from the common strategies.

Currency appears to be an underused asset class. Although the FX market—with nearly USD4 trillion in daily trading volume—is perhaps the largest financial market in the world, assets under management in currency funds (excluding currency overlay programs) may be only USD28 billion. That amount is a small fraction of the estimated USD2 trillion in hedge fund assets. The analytical methodology and empirical evidence presented here suggest that institutional investors should take a new look at whether currency would make a complementary addition to their investment management portfolios.

* * * * * *

The complete monograph can be found at http://www.cfapubs.org/doi/abs/10.2470/rf.v2012.n4.1.

Use your smartphone to scan the QR code to go straight to the webpage.

Equity Valuation and Inflation: A Review (a summary)

Stephen E. Wilcox, CFA
Published 2012 by the Research Foundation of CFA Institute
Summary prepared by Stephen E. Wilcox, CFA

Logic suggests that stock market returns should be neutral to inflation, and history confirms that, over the very long term, they are. Many investors, however, possess short-term horizons and disparage long-term investments as failed short-term ones. Thus, a great deal of the finance literature is dedicated to inflation's short-run impact on returns. Evidence clearly suggests that high and increasing rates of inflation result in a decline in overall market multiples. A deflationary environment has also proved troublesome for equities. The sweet spot for equities seems to be a low and stable rate of inflation.

Real equity returns will be affected by inflation if one or more of the following three conditions exist: (1) Inflation is incorrectly anticipated by market participants; (2) the inflation adjustment for nominal required returns differs from that of nominal growth rates; and (3) expected inflation affects real required returns differently from real growth rates. The literature review proceeds with a discussion of the relevant literature for each of these three violations of inflation neutrality and concludes with an annotated bibliography.

Unexpected Inflation

The inflation rate can be divided into expected and unexpected components. Expected inflation refers to the public's expectation of what inflation will be. If inflation is correctly anticipated and fully reflected in nominal interest rates, the public is less likely to hold non-interest-bearing cash because it loses its purchasing power, and this tends to positively impact equity returns.

In contrast, unanticipated inflation can cause a number of problems for an economy. Uncertainty about future prices increases risk and discourages investment. Income and wealth may also be redistributed because unexpected price increases harm both lenders and savers.

Some of the seminal studies regarding unexpected inflation offer theoretical arguments for an observed negative relationship between unexpected inflation and equity prices. Hypotheses include that this negative relationship is (1) a result of an increased need for companies to raise external financing in the presence of inflation, (2) a market forecast of the detrimental effects inflation will have on future real economic activity and thus on real corporate earnings, (3) a reflection of how inflation and equity prices react to anticipated fiscal and monetary actions, and (4) a consequence of inflation raising the effective tax rate on equity earnings relative to the tax rate on other types of investment income.

The relationship among real economic growth, inflation, and real stock returns has been a topic of empirical interest for a long time. In general, history strongly suggests a positive relationship between real economic growth and real stock returns. But identifying a consistent empirical relationship between inflation and real stock returns has proven difficult, if not impossible. The evidence does suggest, however, that factors such as expectations regarding future real activity, the level of inflation, the source of inflation, and the uncertainty surrounding future inflation affect this relationship.

Money Illusion

The term "money illusion" is most often used to refer to the nominal value of a currency being mistaken for its purchasing power or real value. When a discussion focuses on the effect of money illusion on equity prices, the typical hypothesis is that equity investors suffer from money illusion because they discount real cash flows using nominal discount rates. A real cash flow is a contemporaneous cash flow (such as dividends or earnings) that is priced according to the current period currency value. Nominal discount rates are market rates that reflect expectations regarding future inflation.

If investors suffer from money illusion, then stock markets will become undervalued during periods of high inflation. The logic is that when estimating future cash flows to discount, investors do not fully appreciate the positive effect that inflation will have on nominal earnings. Because this undervaluation should be eliminated once actual nominal cash flows are revealed, high inflation today should ultimately lead to higher future returns. The apparent cheapness of U.S. equities in the late 1970s and their richness in the late 1990s certainly suggest investors suffered from money illusion. Other anecdotal evidence, however, such as U.S. stocks in the 1930s or Japanese stocks in the 1990s, appears contradictory.

It is often argued that a popular valuation model, the Fed model, suffers from money illusion. Using the rationale that bonds and stocks are competing instruments, the model in its simplest form compares the stock market's earnings yield with the yield on a government bond. Stocks are considered undervalued when the earnings yield exceeds the government bond yield and overvalued when it does not.

The Fed model fails to consider that inflation affects reported earnings differently from how it affects the yield on fixed-income securities. The impact of inflation on earnings is spread out over time, due in part to historical cost accounting conventions and lags in price adjustments. In contrast, bond yields adjust very quickly to changes in expected inflation. Thus, the model compares a measure that is mostly real (the earnings yield) with one that is arguably nominal (the government bond yield).

Many empirical studies show that inflation and inflation expectations explain a majority of the time series variation in real equity returns. But some of the literature is supportive of explanations other than money illusion for time periods when changes in the earnings yield and government bond yield are strongly correlated. Evidence also suggests that co-movement can be explained by changes in risk aversion, technology shocks, and the high incidence of stagflation in recent years.

Inflation can cause historical cost-based accounting statements to show illusory profits that mask the true depreciation of capital. A concern is that many investors do not realize that reported earnings are only accounting data and should not necessarily be relied on to make investment decisions. Thus, accounting standard setters have experimented with the requirement that current-cost accounting information be included in financial reports.

Recent evidence suggests that inflation-adjusted accounting variables provide a better explanation of future equity returns than do historical-cost accounting variables. Evidence also shows that the shares of firms that rely heavily on nominal contracts as a funding source appreciate in value relative to the shares of other firms when expected inflation increases. Finally, unrecognized inflation gains and losses have been shown to be useful in predicting abnormal equity returns.

Inflation's Impact on the Real Required Return and Real Growth Rate

A good deal of research has been dedicated to the relationship between inflation and the equity risk premium. The literature is replete with evidence of statistically significant negative relationships between real stock returns and proxies for expected inflation. Unexpected shocks to inflation also appear to be a factor that affects stock market returns. Finally, stock returns of noncyclical industries have been correlated more positively with expected inflation than have those of cyclical industries.

High or unpredictable inflation rates are regarded as economically harmful. They can serve as a drag on productivity and make it difficult for companies to budget or invest for the long term. Evidence does suggest that inflation can result in slower real economic growth, but the relationship appears to be nonlinear.

Some authors have identified structural breaks where high-inflation crises are associated with slow growth, but real GDP appears unaffected at modestly high levels of inflation. The reasons for inflation also appear to affect growth:

Adverse supply shocks have resulted in both slow real growth rates and high inflation rates. The majority of studies show that most economies tend to grow at a faster rate in low or moderate inflation environments.

* * * * * *

The complete literature review, which contains 72 annotated citations on the relevant research, can be found at http://www.cfapubs.org/doi/abs/10.2470/rflr.v7.n1.1.

Use your smartphone to scan the QR code to go straight to the webpage.

The New Field of Liquidity and Financial Frictions (a summary)

David Adler
Published 2012 by the Research Foundation of CFA Institute
Summary prepared by David Adler

In traditional financial models, liquidity does not play a role because it is assumed away: Markets are frictionless, and participants are price takers. But as the 2007–09 crisis in the United States has shown, liquidity in asset pricing is vital for the functioning of financial markets, as well as for the performance of the overall economy.

Liquidity, although it is critical to markets and investing, is nonetheless a slippery concept. There is no universal definition of liquidity in economics, and even when it is well defined, it is hard to measure. Part of the challenge is that the concept of liquidity arises in very different economic contexts: in the ease of trading a security (market liquidity), in the ease of obtaining funding to trade a security (funding liquidity), and finally, in terms of credit in the macroeconomy. Additionally, liquidity can be a flow as well as a stock variable, particularly when the term is used as a synonym for the amount of available credit.

The literature review focuses on three central strands of liquidity research. The first discusses market liquidity and asset pricing. Liquidity-based, asset-pricing models provide insight into the impact of liquidity on the expected returns of numerous asset classes and offer information about the real source of outperformance by the often highly illiquid "endowment" investment model. The second major strand of the literature explains how markets can turn illiquid overnight; many of these theoretical models anticipated the possibility of a liquidity crisis in the United States. The third and most active strand of liquidity research focuses on the interrelated issues of funding liquidity, systemic risk, and the macroeconomic impact of a liquidity crisis.

Understanding liquidity, even if the underlying literature is often highly academic and abstract, should be of great interest to both practitioners and policymakers. This new field has developed a rich set of financial theories that can explain much about the ongoing crisis and also solve many puzzles in finance.

Liquidity and Asset Pricing

The liquidity of an asset affects its price as well as its expected returns. There are two central academic narratives on how liquidity affects asset pricing: Lack of liquidity can be viewed as both a cost and a risk. Investors need to be compensated for both.

Here the word "liquidity" is being used in a market liquidity context—that is, the ease of buying and selling an asset. Market liquidity has three different dimensions: speed (how quickly an asset can be bought or sold), transaction cost (typically measured by the bid–ask spread), and depth, as seen in the potential price impact of a trade. Measuring these different dimensions of liquidity is a specialized subfield of the liquidity literature and is not always straightforward. Some easy-to-use, low-frequency measures are discussed in the literature review.

The case of "restricted" stock provides a very clear example of how the liquidity of an asset affects its price. Restricted stock is highly illiquid in that it cannot trade on public markets for a specified holding period. Restricted stock sold at more than a 30% discount during the 1990s compared with unrestricted stock of the same creditworthy company. There are similar examples from corporate bonds and even Treasuries.

The central intuition behind this strand of the liquidity asset-pricing literature is that because there is a potential transaction cost associated with buying or selling relatively illiquid assets, investors must be compensated for this cost. Investors with long time horizons and without immediate trading needs can accrue returns by holding illiquid assets.

A newer approach in liquidity and asset pricing is to view illiquidity as a risk factor as well as a cost. Liquidity is marketwide and cannot be diversified away; the commonality of liquidity means that traders can become stuck, particularly in times of crisis, regardless of the individual characteristics of a security. Securities are not equally sensitive to these marketwide movements in liquidity, and investors should require those assets that are more sensitive to have higher expected returns.

The academic literature has developed several pricing models of liquidity as a risk factor. The most complete is the liquidity-adjusted capital asset pricing model (L-CAPM). Here, the standard CAPM is augmented with liquidity as a risk factor, or beta. In this model, liquidity risk is refined into three distinct betas related to the covariance of an asset with the overall market's liquidity. Empirically, L-CAPM supports the idea that liquidity is a priced risk factor, and the model explains data better than the traditional CAPM does. (See the literature review for a fuller description of the model.) Another finding is that a stock's liquidity level (liquidity as a characteristic) is not necessarily related to its liquidity risk (price sensitivity to a marketwide liquidity shock).

Liquidity-risk asset-pricing models are not particularly tractable. The academic literature has struggled to quantify liquidity's impact on pricing in relatively illiquid asset classes, such as timber, real estate, or private equity, in part because of data constraints. Nonetheless, the models—and empirical evidence—are highly suggestive that liquidity, as either a cost or a risk, is priced and that lack of liquidity in an asset is associated with higher expected returns. But there is no free lunch: The liquidity crisis of 2007–2009 demonstrated that investors need to carefully consider the source of their returns and the potential for market illiquidity and inability to trade.

Liquidity and the 2007–09 Crisis

Liquidity crises can be best understood as the manifestations of "liquidity spirals." These are negative amplification loops, where a small shock leads to a major market disruption, including the drying up of liquidity. These spirals can explain the fragility of seemingly liquid markets.

The idea of negative amplification loops in economics is not new; it was perhaps first articulated by the economist Irving Fisher. The setup of a liquidity spiral varies from model to model, but all models share the idea that an initial loss on a position causes selling, which leads to a price drop, which leads to more selling, and so on, until the market spirals downward. A key related concept is the idea of funding liquidity. Funding liquidity has various definitions but can be thought of as the ease with which market makers or arbitrageurs can obtain funding. In a liquidity crisis, these market participants face some sort of funding shock, be it tightened margins, uncertainty about the value of collateral used to obtain funding, or mark-to-market markdowns of their assets. In the 2007–09 crisis, funding for major investment banks became constrained when the value of mortgage-backed securities used for collateral became uncertain. Investment banks were unable to fund their positions and were forced to sell many of their assets. They created a negative feedback loop in doing so because all banks were similarly constrained and sold assets at the same time, as plunging mark-to-market values on their balance sheets forced them to delever. Liquidity spirals swept across markets, and a major liquidity crisis ensued.

Post-Crisis Research

The liquidity crisis has sparked a new research agenda that maps out ways to improve financial stability as well as a new understanding of how a banking crisis affects the larger economy. Although it is unknown to most nonspecialists, macro models used by economists and central banks, called dynamic stochastic general equilibrium (DSGE) models, lack a financial sector. The absence of a finance sector in DSGE models reflects the assumptions of frictionless finance and the rarity of previous financial crises and also makes the models more mathematically tractable. Therefore, when the crisis hit, policymakers were left without a model of how to proceed.

The post-crisis liquidity research agenda has many related strands, including ways to measure and mitigate systemic risk and assessments of the possibility of another liquidity crisis. The larger academic approach is to combine macroeconomics with finance—that is, to incorporate finance into macro models. Whereas macro models in the past have focused on the role of expectations, fiscal policy, or monetary policy in economic growth, this newer, developing body of research focuses on the role of credit. A parallel policy agenda is to find ways to improve financial stability and the ability to recover from financial crises.

* * * * * *

The complete literature review, which contains 101 annotated citations on the relevant research, can be found at http://www.cfapubs.org/doi/abs/10.2470/rflr.v7.n2.1.

Use your smartphone to scan the QR code to go straight to the webpage.

The Psychology of Ethics in the Finance and Investment Industry (a summary)

Thomas Oberlechner
Print book published 2007 and audio book published 2012
by the Research Foundation of CFA Institute
Summary prepared by Thomas Oberlechner

A number of characteristics make the finance and investment industry particularly vulnerable to ethical breakdown. Temptations to profit from unethical behavior are larger than in any other field. Professional barriers to entering the investment industry are limited and may be crossed by people from a variety of backgrounds. Increased specialization and complexity can obscure financial actors' views of the consequences of their actions. *The Psychology of Ethics in the Finance and Investment Industry* provides deep and stimulating insight into how professionals consider ethics in their daily decision making and the psychological processes that determine how ethical (and unethical) these decisions are. The book explains how finance and investment professionals can, on the one hand, make morally wrong decisions against their better judgment in crystal clear situations and, on the other hand, act ethically in the midst of conflicting values, temptations, and rewards.

The anonymity of financial transactions generates a psychological setting that facilitates unethical actions. Psychologist Philip Zimbardo conducted an experiment that supports this claim. He abandoned cars with removed license plates and raised hoods in two different social environments, Palo Alto, CA, and the Bronx, NY. Unbeknownst to the passers-by, the cars were filmed from some distance. In the Bronx, it took no more than 10 minutes for the first vandals to begin their work of destruction, and within two days, more than 20 acts of theft or damage were committed. All but one of these acts were committed by adults, many of them well dressed and driving their own cars. In stark contrast, no single act of vandalism was recorded in Palo Alto over the duration of a week. Instead, when the experimenters removed the car, concerned residents informed the police that a car might have been stolen.

According to the neoclassical economic perspective, ethics is simply a behavioral constraint to the actual motivation of egoistic self-interest. Psychological research, however, has shown convincingly that people have an intrinsic interest in being ethical. For example, in the so-called ultimatum game, the first player's task is to divide $10 between himself and the second player. The second player either accepts the offer or declines (in which case both players get nothing).

Although from the viewpoint of economic rationality the second player should thankfully accept even minimal propositions, offers far below $5 are usually rejected because they violate basic values of justice and fairness.

Many actions that are not explicitly prevented by the law cannot be considered ethical, as the example of an investment bank executive allowing his girlfriends to use the corporate jet for personal travel shows. Thus, determining whether something is right or wrong from an ethical viewpoint differs from analyzing it from a legal viewpoint. Moreover, a true understanding of people's actual ethical decision making goes far beyond normative ideals. Psychologists' attempts to understand real-life ethics discriminate between various stages in the ethical decision-making process: (1) identify an ethical dilemma, (2) judge what is ethical, (3) intend to act ethically, and (4) act ethically. Differentiating between these stages explains why investment professionals do not always recognize that a decision they are about to make has a moral component, that their knowing what is morally right does not automatically mean that they intend to do what is morally right, and that their intending to do what is morally right is not the same as their acting on that intention.

"Moral intensity" addresses the extent to which finance and investment professionals perceive an issue to be morally important. Moral intensity is high when the importance of the ethical dimension involved in a situation is clear and when ethical considerations weigh heavily in the decision maker's mind. It is low when the decision maker is hardly aware that a situation has an ethical component. Various psychological factors will determine whether a finance and investment professional considers a situation high or low on moral intensity: (1) The magnitude of consequences addresses the overall harm and benefits that may result from a decision. For example, a fraud scheme that causes thousands of investors to suffer financial losses will be perceived to be of greater magnitude than an act that causes only a few investors to suffer a loss. (2) Social consensus expresses the level of social agreement that a certain act is morally right or wrong. For example, insider trading is regarded as unethical in the United States with higher social consensus than in Japan. (3) The probability of effect indicates the likelihood that a behavior will lead to harm. When a financial analyst coats a negative outlook on a company's stock performance in soft language, the probability of effect depends on how likely it is that investors will actually be misled by these euphemistic labels. (4) Temporal immediacy asks how much time there is between the unethical behavior and its harmful consequences. When consequences are in the distant future, people perceive less ethical urgency in the decision they are presently taking. (5) Proximity indicates how psychologically close decision makers feel to the people who experience the disadvantage and harm of their unethical behavior. For example, unethical and illegal "front running" involves more proximity when the customer is somebody frequently seen at social dinners. (6) Concentration of effect addresses whether the same harm is spread thinly over many people or whether it affects only a few people in a concentrated way. For example, although the resulting overall damage may be equal, a fraudulent transaction from the account of one individual client has a greater concentration of effect than a fraud scheme based on incorrectly rounding small digits after the decimal in all client accounts.

Traditional explanations of unethical decision making have focused either on characteristics of the individual (the "bad apples" approach) or on the nature of the social and organizational environment (the "bad barrels" approach). Psychology looks at these factors in interaction: A full understanding of ethics involves the interplay of characteristics and behavior at both individual and social (both organizational and market) levels. Regarding individual ethics, psychology sheds light on how finance and investment professionals develop and change their ethical convictions and belief systems. Psychologist Lawrence Kohlberg describes moral development as progressing through a sequence of stages of moral reasoning. This moral or ethical reasoning may be the most important factor determining finance and investment professionals' implicit understanding of what means "good" and what means "bad," ethically, and how they resolve moral dilemmas.

Kohlberg separates moral development into three levels: pre-conventional, conventional, and post-conventional. On the pre-conventional level, individuals think about ethical questions in terms of their own welfare; ethics is based on self-interest. Individuals define right and wrong simply depending on external punishments and rewards.

On the conventional level, people primarily consider the expectations of others to determine what is right. Behavior that is consistent with the expectations of others is considered ethical. Acceptance and approval by others, and loyalty to the social environment, are essential. People strive to be "good boys" or "nice girls" to please others and win their approval, or they think in terms of law and order, where to be ethical means to dutifully obey society's laws.

Only on the post-conventional level do people reach full ethical maturity. They reason that laws and rules should be followed is because they promote the welfare of society. Laws should be followed not simply because they are the law but because these laws are established by mutual agreement and serve the benefit of all. Moreover, when people have developed the highest capacity to think about ethics, they are able to look beyond society and autonomously develop complex notions of fairness, justice, compassion, and equality.

Next to these developmental differences, Machiavellianism describes a general tendency to deceive and manipulate others for personal gain. Machiavellian personalities are highly manipulative, pragmatic, and persuasive;

they believe that whichever means is needed to achieve a desired end is justified. High degrees of Machiavellianism lead to unethical decisions. In contrast, moral imagination describes an individual's ability to perceive a variety of options for behaving in a given situation and to imagine ethically good and bad consequences of these options. People with high moral imagination reflect about decisions with moral implications flexibly and in complex ways. These traits and other implicit processes in the individual—such as attitudes (which are often not conscious), heuristics (which reduce and simplify the existing information by psychological shortcuts and rules of thumb), and cognitive dissonance reduction (a reaction to contradictory perceptions and attitudes)—go a long way in explaining unethical behavior on the individual level.

Moreover, even otherwise-ethical finance and investment professionals may use rationalization strategies that compromise their sense of ethics by morally "disengaging" from their unethical behavior. These strategies include a change in finance professionals'

- perception of the unethical behavior, which is achieved by creating moral justifications for their behavior, by giving unethical behavior euphemistic labels, or by soothing comparisons;
- perception of the damaging consequences of the unethical behavior, which is achieved by completely closing one's eyes to the consequences, by playing down the consequences, or by distorting the consequences;
- awareness of being responsible for the connection between the blameworthy behavior and its damaging consequences, which is achieved by displacing responsibility onto others or by diffusing responsibility among many; and
- perspective of the victims of the unethical behavior, which is achieved by dehumanizing the victims or even by putting the blame on the victim.

In addition to these individual explanations of unethical behavior, situational factors can lead to radical differences in the ethics of behavior. Situational factors have been tested by social psychological experiments. In one such experiment, everyday people willingly administered what they believed to be extremely painful and life-threatening electric shocks to others when ordered to do so by someone in a position of authority; in another, participants quickly took on the roles of psychologically cruel and sadistic prison guards when placed in positions of considerable power. It is hard to overestimate the implications of these experiments on decision making in finance and investment because they shed light on the collective practices of individuals in financial organizations—that go against the law and violate fundamental professional rules.

Rather than thinking and deciding as individuals, finance and investment professionals are always members of groups, organizations, and the investment community. Among all the psychological processes influencing the ethics of individuals in groups, conformity is the most basic and pervasive. The ethical beliefs, attitudes, decisions, and standards of people who interact with each other in a group have a tendency to converge, often until they are practically identical. But psychologists have also observed that group interaction produces group polarization. The dangerous influence of these processes on the ethics of decision making has been shown in the verdicts reached by collectively biased panels of judges in juries. Conformity also has a dramatic effect on the ethics in the decisions taken by finance and investment professionals. When these decisions result from group processes, they are likely to reflect a systematically different set of ethics. "Groupthink," first described by psychologist Irving Janis, leads group members to become less realistic in their opinions, less efficient with their intellectual resources, and less demanding in their moral standards. Groups of finance and investment professionals who are affected by groupthink develop a false illusion that they are invulnerable, and the overconfidence embedded in this illusion may lead them to take excessive risks. Warnings are collectively discounted and rationalized away. Moreover, a misleading sense of unanimity in the group emerges both from group members who self-censor possible doubts and deviations from the seeming group consensus and from the pressure on group members attempting to dissent from this consensus. Most importantly, group members develop an unquestioned belief in the group's own morality. This belief leads members to pay no attention to the ethical implications of the group's decisions, and it leads members to withhold from the group any information that could challenge the group's self-complacent certainty about the ethics of its decisions.

Some psychological aspects of ethics are of particular importance to leaders and organizations in finance and investment, including the consequences of power for ethics in investment organizations and the requirements of ethical leadership. Measures that help ensure an organizational culture of ethics include codes of conduct, ethics officers and ombudspersons, and ethics committees. When organizational leaders cross ethical or legal borders, futile attempts to counter their actions may result in whistle blowing. It is the ethical responsibility of, and also in the interests of, financial institutions to provide employees with mechanisms that allow them to react quickly and without fear of retaliation to wrong and illegal behavior within the organization, especially abuses by those higher in power and authority.

Compensation and reward systems are among the most relevant determinants of ethical behavior in organizations. These systems are a direct reflection of organizational ethics and of underlying organizational values, but their effects often contradict the espoused values of financial and investment organizations. Far too frequently, organizations reward unwanted behaviors and actively discourage ethical behavior by the monetary incentives they establish. Moreover, implicit reward systems shape the (un)ethical behavior of financial and investment professionals. Such implicit rewards are found, for example, in promotion processes. The questions of who is favored by the supervisor and who gets promoted (and with what kind of ethical track record) are critical because these people will be models shaping the behavior of other employees.

The ethics of financial and investment organizations can be strengthened through education and training programs. Sound ethics training and education programs should increase finance professionals' awareness of actual ethical issues, provide participants with practical frameworks, create a climate conducive to learning, focus on concrete and relevant issues, establish clear links to the company's ethics guidelines and codes of conduct, and include a follow-up to the training sessions. Although ethics training and education cannot convert morally corrupt individuals, they can certainly raise awareness for ethical concerns in investment companies and improve the ethical decision making of professionals.

"The line separating good and evil passes through every human heart," Russian writer and Nobel Laureate Aleksandr Solzhenitsyn once said. *The Psychology of Ethics in the Finance and Investment Industry* provides an informative and stimulating understanding of this dividing line that lies at the core of each financial and investment professional, of each investment organization, and of the financial industry itself.

* * * * * *

The complete monograph can be found at http://www.cfapubs.org/doi/abs/10.2470/rf.v2007.n2.4697.

Use your smartphone to scan the QR code to go straight to the webpage.

Good Derivatives: A Story of Financial and Environmental Innovation (a summary)

Richard L. Sandor
Presentation to the 11th Annual Research for the Practitioner Workshop, 6 May 2012
Summary prepared by Richard L. Sandor

Financial Innovation

Financial innovation, in general, and the derivatives market, specifically, have been the subject of blistering attacks since the Great Recession of 2008. Paul Volcker, one of the leading central bankers of our time, recently quipped, "The most important financial innovation that I have seen in the past 20 years is the ATM." The Nobel Prize–winning economist Joseph Stiglitz said he "could not find any social good in complex derivatives."

Compared with other innovations, financial innovation is often overlooked or misunderstood by both the general population and many professional economists. Henry Ford is widely acclaimed for his contribution to innovations in mass production. But few even recognize the name Luca Pacioli, the 15th-century Italian mathematician who documented the procedure for the double-entry bookkeeping system, which became the foundation for modern accounting. Kenneth Arrow, another Nobel Prize–winning economist, has rightly argued that such innovations as the limited liability corporation and double-entry bookkeeping are as important to humankind as the invention of the steam engine and the semiconductor. Financial innovations allow markets to exist where they did not exist before. Why, then, have they gotten so little attention and appreciation from economists and the public?

Financial innovations are often overlooked for at least three reasons: (1) They are intangible and thus may be difficult to understand; (2) they tend to be "wholesale," meaning they are not part of the retail mass market; and (3) they are often collaborative and complex and, therefore, have no obvious owners. Furthermore, until recently, they were not patentable and their benefits accrued mostly to first movers.

Newly organized markets are often combinations of financial, legal, and social innovations that emanate from fundamental economic and social structural changes. These markets have to be invented; they do not just magically appear. They also have to be nurtured; an institutional framework has to be built to support their development. In the past 40 years, certain types of financial innovations—what we call "good derivatives"—have been a positive force in value creation. These new markets are now expanding to address pollution, thus providing new challenges and opportunities for finance professionals.

"Good Derivatives"

Good derivatives are those listed on regulated exchanges plus those that are effectively self-regulated. They are transparent and perform an important risk management function by preventing the systemic breakdown of financial institutions and capital markets. The transparency of futures prices, options on futures, and options on securities on regulated exchanges results in lower transaction costs in the purchase and sale of commodities, stocks, bonds, and other instruments.

These good derivatives have grown dramatically in the past 40 years. In 1970, 13.7 million derivatives contracts were traded in the United States, and in 1975, the U.S. derivatives market constituted 93% of worldwide volume. By 2010, 22.3 *billion* contracts were traded on more than 78 derivatives exchanges in 36 countries. New derivatives and new exchanges were responsible for almost all of the growth in futures and options markets over the past 40 years. The compounded annual growth rate in the volume of futures and options traded was over 18% for the 40-year period from 1970 to 2010. The industry doubled every 3.9 years, which far surpassed the growth in the number of airline passengers or the number of automobiles produced during the same period. Futures and options that did not exist in 1970 now constitute 79.8% of the volume on organized exchanges in the United States.

These markets grew because of new products, and they were reinforced recently by the advent of electronic trading. In 1970, there were no currency derivatives, no stock options, no interest rates, no equity indices, and no energy-related products. There were no exchange-traded funds (ETFs) in the equity world. Each product drove another wave of innovation. Forty years later, it is hard to imagine that at one time these products did not even exist. The combined market capitalization of U.S. derivatives exchanges—Chicago Mercantile Exchange (CME), Intercontinental Exchange (ICE), and Chicago Board Options Exchange (CBOE)—is around $35 billion, bigger than the total market capitalization of the top five U.S. airlines ($24 billion).

Benefits of Good Derivatives

No regulated exchanges required government bailouts during the Great Recession of 2008. Good derivatives performed flawlessly. These regulated and transparent markets performed a risk-transfer function. The clearing and margining functions provided by exchanges also significantly lowered counterparty risk, thus minimizing systemic risk. The transparency these markets provide has subsidiary benefits, reflected in the prices in primary markets. As spreads narrow in the futures market, enormous liquidity benefits are generated in the spot markets (i.e., lower transaction costs). These markets also have an impact on price discovery, affecting the price forecast for crops, metals, bonds, short-term interest rates, and equity indices. They also serve an intertemporal price discovery function. For example, futures prices on such crops as soybeans, corn, and cotton provide a signal to farmers on what to plant.

The aforementioned functions are enabled by speculation. This statement will likely be controversial, but speculation is a good thing if it is regulated and controlled. Speculation and gambling are different. In the case of gambling, there is no risk until you build the race track or the casino. Its risk is manufactured for leisure purposes. In speculation, the risk predates the existence of speculative institutions: Soybean prices, stocks, and interest rates go up and down whether or not there is a way to hedge these price risks. The questions are, Who assumes the risk and for how long, and at what cost is the risk transfer achieved?

Perhaps the biggest speculators in the world are the private equity and venture capital firms that have seeded many of our biggest innovations. We didn't seem to get upset when Apple and Facebook shifted their financial risks to outside investors and focused on managing their comparative advantage, which is to take technological risks and develop new products. Speculators in derivatives markets are in essence no different from those who provided capital to all of the new startups that have made Silicon Valley the success it is today.

Every day, hundreds of thousands of entities and individuals transact and clear more than a trillion dollars in value in over 75 regulated exchanges worldwide. These regulated and transparent markets bring many buyers and sellers together in a single place. They create enormous value by facilitating price discovery and risk mitigation on products ranging from government debt and mortgages to transportation, food, and the environment. The ability to bring all these buyers and sellers together has considerably lowered the costs of doing business for many market participants. It has had a direct, positive impact on the lives of millions of people around the world either by making housing affordable, lowering food and transportation prices, or democratizing access to credit for small businesses.

Government National Mortgage Association (GNMA) futures, the first financial futures regulated by the U.S. Commodity Futures Trading Commission (CFTC), provide an example of the benefits of good derivatives. The formation of the GNMA enabled the "bundling" of small loans into securities to be collateralized by the Federal Housing Administration/Veteran's Administration (FHA/VA) and backed by the U.S. government. The GNMA provided efficient and homogeneous evidence of ownership and a conveyance vehicle, which ultimately evolved into spot and forward markets. The bid–ask spread was two points in the market in 1970. The bonds were 98 bid offered at 100. By 1973, the spreads collapsed to one point, and in 1974, they collapsed to three-quarters of a point. Ultimately, the GNMA ("Ginnie Mae") futures contract was launched at the Chicago Board of Trade (CBOT) in 1975. Within three weeks, the spread started to narrow in the spot, forward, and futures markets; after less than six months, it reached 1/32 of a point in the futures as well as the OTC spot and forward markets. In practical terms, the collapse of the GNMA spread from three-quarters of a point to a 32nd means that the average American pays $6,000 less over the life of his or her mortgage. That is a big difference.

In the case of the 10-year note, in 1982 it traded within an eighth- to a quarter-point spread. The collapse of the spread from an eighth or a quarter to a 32nd or half of a 32nd represented $500 million less in interest costs to the U.S. government. To anyone investing in 10-year notes, it saved $10 billion in transaction costs, which translated into gains for retirees, homeowners, and pensioners. Therefore, it is very important to talk about transaction costs and liquidity in terms of these examples so that regulators, the media, and the public can easily understand the positive impact good derivatives have had.

Environmental Markets: The Next Good Derivatives

The same impact in terms of improving health and living conditions was experienced with the rise of environmental derivatives, which we believe are the next growth area. In the 1980s, the United States had a major problem with acid rain. The problem resulted from the burning of coal by utilities in the U.S. Midwest, and those emissions were drifting toward the northeast coast. The Clean Air Act Amendments (CAAA) of 1990 came up with an innovative concept called "cap and trade." To show how this works, let's say that a regulation lowers permitted emissions across the board by 10%. It could be that Utility A is a lot better than Utility B at reducing pollution and could make reductions of 20% to 30% because it can modify its boilers and change the way it burns fossil fuels. Utility B cannot change because it has physical or technological constraints.

In this case, Utility B will buy the excess reductions from Utility A and satisfy the reduction requirements, and society will be better off. Through this process, emissions will be reduced with the least cost to the economy.

How well did the program do? The U.S. Environmental Protection Agency (EPA) Acid Rain Program, enabled by the CAAA, facilitated the reduction of SO_2 emissions by 64% at a fraction of the forecasted cost. Independent estimates by the EPA show a 40:1 benefit-to-cost ratio. In 2010 alone, acid rain–related health care costs were reduced by $123 billion at a cost of somewhere between $1 billion and $3 billion. Between 20,000 and 50,000 lives were saved in that year too. This is the poster case of how markets can deal with environmental problems; acid rain has disappeared as a problem in the United States. However, "cap and trade" has a negative connotation among our leaders, despite the fact that the United States established what is still to this day the most successful cap-and-trade system in the world.

Following the initial success of the Acid Rain Program and our experience with the program, our firm (Environmental Financial Products, EFP) became involved in the process of designing market mechanisms to address another environmental problem—the growing accumulation of carbon emissions in the atmosphere, widely believed to contribute to climate change.

Our approach at EFP was to design and develop a private program, and we looked at it the same way that we looked at all financial innovations. That is, we had to look at the gains from trade, and then we looked at the costs. The latter represent the institutional costs of setting up the market and involve legislative and regulatory costs as well as the costs of transacting. We have to minimize these costs, and they have to be less than the gains. We started a voluntary market for carbon called the Chicago Climate Exchange (CCX), where members (corporations, municipalities, and universities) committed to a 6% reduction in their greenhouse gas emissions. CCX members represented 17% of the Dow Jones Industrial Average (DJIA), 11% of the Fortune 100, and 20% of the largest CO_2-emitting utilities in the United States. CCX's total membership reached a size where its output was approximately 600 million metric tons of CO_2 equivalents, making it a "country" larger than Germany in terms of emissions subject to a cap. The members cut emissions by 400 million tons—80 percent of what France emits in a year.

Price can be a catalyst for change. CCX carbon traded at a dollar or two per ton. We had a project in the south Indian state of Kerala where rural communities used organic waste as a renewable source for clean cooking fuel and heating. Three thousand rural poor participated in the program, selling the carbon credits associated with this project into the CCX market and initially making about $24 per family. The market incentive also prevented girls from having to forage for firewood, allowing them to go to school and providing improved cooking conditions. The program expanded annually and subsequently reached 100,000 rural poor all over India. An ancillary institutional framework involving the creation of a "carbon currency" was developed, allowing people to exchange these credits for cash at local banks or use vouchers to purchase groceries. It is clear that in a regulated and transparent environment, price signals can change lives. They have the power not only to allocate capital but also to bring about social change.

Food for Thought

I have talked about how the past 40 years have shaped finance. Now is the time to identify three issues that could affect this industry for the next 40 years.

The first issue is regulation. We believe in regulation, having spent 40 years in a regulated environment. But we also believe in good regulation. The U.S. Constitution is six pages long. The bill creating the U.S. Federal Reserve is 25 pages. The bill creating the CFTC is 150 pages. The Dodd–Frank Wall Street Reform and Consumer Protection Act of 2010 is over 2,000 pages. It does not seem reasonable that 2,000 pages are required to regulate banks when it took just 25 to establish the Fed.

The second issue is credit rating agencies. Are credit rating agencies a cure or a problem? Is it a good model when companies pay someone to rate them? Will the results be accurate? A look at some facts may be telling. In the United States, there are only four AAA rated companies. In the world, only 14 countries have a AAA rating. However, from 2000 to 2008, Moody's and S&P rated almost 17,000 securities as AAA. This pattern and model deserve better scrutiny.

The third issue pertains to the insurance industry. The United States is a $16 trillion economy, but only $550 billion of insurance company capital is available to deal with all of the property and casualty risks associated with earthquakes, hurricanes, tornadoes, and floods. Storms like Hurricane Sandy, which severely affected New York, have the potential to wipe out the entire capital of the insurance industry. The capital requirements in the property and casualty business demand increased attention. The potential impact on the bond and stock markets when the next catastrophe occurs could be devastating. Unfortunately, no one seems to be paying attention to this problem, given the expectation that states and the federal government will always stand ready to pay the bill.

The Future

Cap and trade is now being adopted around the world. Europe is the leader and is the home of the largest and most mature market. China and such other emerging nations as India and Brazil have become places to watch in this new sphere of financial innovation. The Chinese have been studying emissions markets for well over a decade now. They have been quietly developing the human and institutional capacity that could allow them to launch one of the largest domestic environmental markets. It would rival the current European Union market in size of emissions as well as offer a potential counterpoint to the world's other main emitter, the United States. The Chinese have established seven pilot programs around the country, with five cities and two provinces receiving the approval of the central government to experiment with emissions markets. Moreover, such countries as Australia and South Korea have passed enabling legislation for cap and trade.

Finally, water as an asset class holds great promise. The market is still nascent, and many of the critical ingredients are emerging. The reporting and benchmarking of corporate water use are helpful first steps in quantifying the water footprints of corporations. Water indices and sustainable stock indices incorporating water risks are being developed.

As water markets emerge, we should incorporate lessons from the development of other good derivatives. By this, we mean that the market should be developed in a transparent and regulated derivatives exchange-based system with centralized clearing. This is even more critical for water, given its life-sustaining role. Caution needs to be applied to ensure that the basic human right to water will not be threatened by faulty designs. Pilot programs will prove invaluable in furthering the knowledge base and allowing for a flexible and practical approach. The implications from a water crisis may be universal, but we should not forget that water still is very much a regional issue. Recognizing the interests of regional stakeholders will be unavoidable if a successful market is to emerge.

Regulated and transparent markets can also have a positive impact on addressing other externalities in areas such as R&D, medicine, and education.

Conclusion

The rapidly growing field of environmental finance includes the set of financial innovations that make use of market-based mechanisms to address air pollution and, increasingly, water quality and scarcity issues. These emerging markets and the extended use of these other policy tools are introducing fundamental changes to the global business environment. Businesses today have to be alert and prepare for new types of corporate risks related to the environment and natural resources. In addition, corporations also have to be aware of the opportunities these environmental markets have to offer. Environmental markets now exist for a variety of environmental commodities, including emission credits, renewable energy credits, and sustainable equity indices. These financial innovations allow businesses to simultaneously realize major new commercial opportunities while achieving their stated energy and environmental goals. They also hold the promise of an expanded role for financial analysts.

In short, we are witnessing a major fusion and unique convergence of financial and environmental markets, and this fusion is here to stay. This transition will eventually change asset management and redefine the role of markets in addressing environmental and social problems. Derivatives are like hammers: They can be used to destroy or to build. Finance professionals have a unique opportunity in the 21st century to use these tools to continue to build environmentally sound markets.

* * * * * *

The video webcast can be found at http://www.cfainstitute.org/learning/products/multimedia/Pages/69956.aspx.

Use your smartphone to scan the QR code to go straight to the webpage.

Rethinking the Equity Risk Premium (a summary)

Elroy Dimson, FSIP
Presentation to the 11th Annual Research for the Practitioner Workshop, 6 May 2012[1]
Summary prepared by Elroy Dimson

The equity risk premium is the *expected future* difference between the total return on a stock index and the total return on a risk-free investment. It is the most important number in finance for a number of reasons:

- It is a forecast of future equity returns.
- It guides asset allocation.
- It determines the cost of capital.
- It is central to valuing companies and stocks.
- It is crucial to project appraisal.
- It indicates fair returns in regulated industries.

Yet, there is no general consensus on the size of the equity premium. The range of equity premium estimates published in influential textbooks is astonishingly wide, in recent years spanning between 3% and 10% per year.

To get a better estimate, we were thus motivated to (1) look back and see what equity premium had been realized over a long historical period and (2) determine what adjustments, if any, need to be made to such a historical measure for use as a guide to the future.

In the context of the capital asset pricing model of Sharpe (1964) and others, the equity premium posits a relationship between the amount of risk taken and the expected return of an asset or portfolio. In other words, the equity premium is the market price of risk. The current time frame, in which real (inflation-adjusted) yields on long-term government bonds are essentially zero, is unusual in that the equity premium is essentially the *only* source of real returns on assets.

[1]This talk focused on an article I wrote with Paul Marsh and Mike Staunton (Dimson, Marsh, and Staunton 2011). We are grateful to CFA Institute for the opportunity given to me to present our analysis at a number of venues in the United States and Europe.

Historical Returns (1900–2012)

In 2002, we published the book *Triumph of the Optimists* (Dimson, Marsh, and Staunton 2002), in which we documented the fact that equity returns had been much higher than bond returns over the historical period from 1900 to the present. This finding was true for all the countries for which such a long data series was available, and it remains true for the period 1900–2012 in the expanded group of markets in the latest update of our research (Dimson, Marsh, and Staunton 2013a). The goal was to compile a definitive global history of capital market returns, including data for stocks, bonds, bills, inflation, currency, and GDP. We now cover 22 countries: the principal market economies of Europe; the United States and Canada; Australia, New Zealand, and Japan; South Africa; and two countries (Russia and China) that experienced a long interruption in their financial systems.

In every country, for the 1900–2012 period, equities beat inflation *and* bonds *and* bills. Real total returns on equities ranged from less than 1% in Austria and just under 2% in Italy to more than 7% in South Africa and Australia. The equity risk premium, measured relative to U.S. Treasury bills, ranged from just under 3% in Denmark to over 6% in South Africa and Australia. The U.S. equity premium was 5.3% for this period, and the market-value-weighted world average equity premium was 4.1%. Although the world average is close to the U.S. number, partly because of the large weight of the United States in the world portfolio, it is perhaps surprising that the United States is not more clearly superior to other countries given its outstanding economic performance. Our work shows that equities have been a superior investment wherever markets have been continuously functioning, not just in the *ex post* best-performing countries.

A closer look at the United States and United Kingdom is in order. In the United States, a dollar invested in a stock market total return index in 1900, and adjusted for inflation, grew by the end of 2012 to $952, whereas a dollar similarly invested in bonds and bills grew to $9.45 and $2.75, respectively. In the United Kingdom, thc corresponding results for a pound invested in 1900 are £316 for equities and £5.46 and £2.85 for bonds and bills, respectively.

Components of the Historical Returns

We then looked to see what factors influenced these returns. We distinguished between nominal and real currency returns. The nominal currency return is just the change in the home-currency value of the foreign currency; the real currency return adjusts that number for the inflation differential between the two countries so that changes in currency values caused solely by inflation differences are not counted. Although nominal currencies were quite volatile, this variability mostly reflected inflation differences, so real currency returns were surprisingly stable, with no country experiencing more than 1% annual real currency appreciation or depreciation. (Switzerland had the best-performing currency, and Austria, the worst.) Thus, an investor would have earned roughly the same equity risk premium, on average, across countries, whether or not she had hedged her currency exposure.

Dividends matter. Most of the real total return from holding equities was from the dividend. If dividends are removed from the 952:1 cumulative real growth of a dollar invested in U.S. stocks for the 1900–2012 period, the growth shrinks to 9:1 (a compound growth rate of 2.0% per year instead of 6.3%). The comparable data for the United Kingdom show the 316:1 cumulative real growth shrinking to below 2:1 (a compound growth rate of 0.6% instead of 5.2%).

The concern is that today, dividend yields are much lower than they were on average historically. By definition, the equity risk premium is equal to the dividend yield, plus the real dividend growth rate, plus (minus) expansion (contraction) in the price/dividend ratio, minus the risk-free interest rate. Thus, all other things being equal, a lower dividend yield means a lower forward-looking equity risk premium. This analysis also suggests that real total returns on equities could be lower in the future than they were historically.

Time Variation and Predictability in the Equity Risk Premium

To see whether there is any predictability in the equity risk premium, we first looked at a naïve market-timing strategy. Noting that the 3–3½% expected premium versus bills is only an average, with the actual equity premium expected to vary over time, we hypothesized that at times of market distress, investors are poorer, risk aversion is greater, and the amount of risk in the market is higher. Logically, under such conditions, investors should require higher returns than during easy times. But did they actually experience higher returns?

The results are inconclusive. The five-year realized equity premium (over bills) was, on average, 5.5% after the worst one-fifth of the years, compared with 4.9% over the best one-fifth of the years. The difference is in the predicted direction, but it is not large. It would be difficult to make any money using such a crude timing approach.

We also investigated whether we could pick winning markets cross-sectionally (that is, across national markets at a given point in time). Here, the results are more encouraging. Dividend yield gives a good indication of future return. A strategy that sorts markets into five groups or portfolios by their dividend yields, with periodic rebalancing, would have produced a 13.3% compound annual return for the highest-yielding quintile, compared with 5.4% for the lowest-yielding quintile. For the entire period spanned by our study, this difference adds up to a mountainous variation in final wealth: over $1 million versus under $400 per original dollar invested. This result is a manifestation of the well-known value effect. Furthermore, this dividend-based market rotation strategy worked in each 25-year subperiod. Note that this result ignores transaction costs and also contains hindsight bias, in that it uses a variable that we know after the fact was effective at sorting winners from losers.

Selecting markets based on favoring countries with recent GDP growth did not work well. The countries with slower GDP growth actually beat those with faster growth, but the effect is not large, except after 1972 in an expanded 83-country sample. One possible reason is that faster recent GDP growth means that the stock market is already bid up in anticipation of continued fast growth in corporate earnings, which then (on average) fail to match investors' optimistic projections.

Picking stock markets based on currency strength had interesting outcomes. Countries with currencies that had been weaker over the previous five years had better equity returns than those with recently strong currencies. In the expanded 83-country sample for 1972 to the present, the difference was very large, with weak-currency countries returning 30% annually, compared with 11% for strong-currency countries.

Should Equity Investors be Optimists about the Future?

We called our 2002 book *Triumph of the Optimists* because markets enable optimists and pessimists to place bets against one another. For the 1900–2001 period, and also (although at a slightly diminished rate) for the 1900–2012 period, the optimists won: Equities greatly outpaced fixed-income assets as well as inflation. Maybe the optimists simply got lucky in the 20th century. Alternatively, a natural consequence of the way risks are apportioned between investors is that stocks can be expected to beat less-risky assets over the long haul. Because there are logical reasons why equity investors should earn higher returns than fixed-income investors, we expect this pattern to continue, but at a somewhat slower rate than in the spectacularly successful 20th century. Specifically, we expect a 3–3½% equity risk premium in the future, below the worldwide premium of 4.1% that we report in our most recent publications.

BIBLIOGRAPHY

Dimson, Elroy, Paul Marsh, and Mike Staunton. 2002. *Triumph of the Optimists: 101 Years of Global Investment Returns.* Princeton, NJ: Princeton University Press.

———. 2011. "Equity Premiums around the World." In *Rethinking the Equity Risk Premium.* Edited by P. Brett Hammond, Jr., Martin L. Leibowitz, and Laurence B. Siegel. Charlottesville, VA: Research Foundation of CFA Institute.

———. 2013a. *Credit Suisse Global Investment Returns Yearbook 2013.* Zurich: Credit Suisse Research Institute: www.tinyurl.com/CSgiry2013.

———. 2013b. *Credit Suisse Global Investment Returns Sourcebook 2013.* Zurich: Credit Suisse Research Institute.

Sharpe, William F. 1964. "Capital Asset Prices: A Theory of Market Equilibrium under Conditions of Risk." *Journal of Finance*, vol. 19, no. 3 (September):425–442.

* * * * * *

The video webcast can be found at http://www.cfainstitute.org/learning/products/multimedia/Pages/67696.aspx.

Use your smartphone to scan the QR code to go straight to the webpage.

James R. Vertin Award

The James R. Vertin Award is presented periodically to recognize individuals who have produced a body of research notable for its relevance and enduring value to investment professionals. This award was established in 1996 to honor James R. Vertin, CFA, for his outstanding leadership in promoting excellence and relevancy in research and education.

2012 Vertin Award Winner

Elroy Dimson
Visiting Professor of Finance at Cambridge Judge Business School
Emeritus Professor of Finance at London Business School

There are very few who can boast giving their name to a statistical technique. Elroy Dimson, after whom the "Dimson beta" is named, is one of those few. The Dimson beta measures the risk of infrequently traded securities, and his estimation procedure was one of his first projects as a PhD student in the 1970s. In the 1980s, he went on to design the FTSE Index. Yet Professor Dimson cites a different achievement as his greatest: "*Triumph of the Optimists* is my greatest achievement," he says (referring to his 2002 book and the annual update published by Credit Suisse). "We consider returns from 1900 to the present day across all asset classes in 22 major markets. It underpins the investment strategy of many funds around the world." Ultimately, this study led to him taking the chair of the Strategy Council for the Norwegian Government Pension Fund—the world's largest sovereign wealth fund. He also researches endowment asset management, co-directs long-term investment courses for endowments and foundations at Yale University and the University of Cambridge, and is the co-author of a study of the investment record of the economist John Maynard Keynes. For his next project, he is working with the Norwegian government on long-term sustainable and ethical investment strategies.

Past Vertin Award Winners

2010 Roger Clarke
2009 Robert Shiller
2008 Keith Ambachtsheer
2007 Campbell R. Harvey
2006 Clifford S. Asness
2005 Andrew W. Lo
2004 Edwin J. Elton
2004 Martin Gruber
2003 Barr Rosenberg
2002 William L. Fouse, CFA
2001 Rex A. Sinquefield
2001 Roger G. Ibbotson
2000 Peter L. Bernstein
1998 Martin L. Leibowitz
1997 Jack L. Treynor
1996 William F. Sharpe

Research Foundation Leadership Circle Inductees

The Research Foundation Leadership Circle honors investment professionals whose outstanding commitment and contributions have benefited the Research Foundation of CFA Institute over an extended period of time. In 2012, the Research Foundation was honored to announce the following members of the inaugural class of the Leadership Circle.

Gary Brinson, CFA

George Noyes, CFA

Walter Stern, CFA

James R. Vertin, CFA

RESEARCH FOUNDATION CONTRIBUTION FORM

☑ **Yes**, I want the Research Foundation to continue to fund innovative research that advances the investment management profession. Please accept my tax-deductible contribution at the following level:

Thought Leadership Circle ....US$1,000,000 or more
Named Endowment ....US$100,000 to US$999,999
Research Fellow .... US$10,000 to US$99,999
Contributing Donor .... US$1,000 to US$9,999
Friend .... Up to US$999

I would like to donate $ ____________________.

☐ My check is enclosed (payable to the Research Foundation of CFA Institute).
☐ I would like to donate appreciated securities (send me information).
☐ Please charge my donation to my credit card.
☐ VISA ☐ MC ☐ Amex ☐ Diners ☐ Corporate ☐ Personal

| | | | | | | | | | | | | | | | |
Card Number

___/___ Expiration Date

________________________ Name on card PLEASE PRINT

☐ Corporate Card
☐ Personal Card

________________________ Signature

☐ This is a pledge. Please bill me for my donation of $ ______________
☐ I would like recognition of my donation to be:
☐ Individual donation ☐ Corporate donation ☐ Different individual

____
PLEASE PRINT NAME OR COMPANY NAME AS YOU WOULD LIKE IT TO APPEAR

PLEASE PRINT ☐ Mr. ☐ Mrs. ☐ Ms. MEMBER NUMBER________________

____
Last Name (Family Name) First Middle Initial

____
Title

____
Address

____
City State/Province Countr y ZIP/Postal Code

Please mail this completed form with your contribution to:
The Research Foundation of CFA Institute • P.O. Box 2082
Charlottesville, VA 22902-2082 USA

For more on the Research Foundation of CFA Institute, please visit www.cfainstitute.org/about/foundation/.

Named Endowments

The Research Foundation of CFA Institute acknowledges with sincere gratitude the generous contributions of the Named Endowment participants listed below.

Gifts of at least US$100,000 qualify donors for membership in the Named Endowment category, which recognizes in perpetuity the commitment toward unbiased, practitioner-oriented, relevant research that these firms and individuals have expressed through their generous support of the Research Foundation of CFA Institute.

Ameritech
Anonymous
Robert D. Arnott
Theodore R. Aronson, CFA
Asahi Mutual Life
Batterymarch Financial Management
Boston Company
Boston Partners Asset Management, L.P.
Gary P. Brinson, CFA
Brinson Partners, Inc.
Capital Group International, Inc.
Concord Capital Management
Dai-Ichi Life Company
Daiwa Securities
Mr. and Mrs. Jeffrey Diermeier
Gifford Fong Associates
Investment Counsel Association of America, Inc.
Jacobs Levy Equity Management
John A. Gunn, CFA
Jon L. Hagler Foundation
Long-Term Credit Bank of Japan, Ltd.
Lynch, Jones & Ryan
Meiji Mutual Life Insurance Company
Miller Anderson & Sherrerd, LLP
John B. Neff, CFA
Nikko Securities Co., Ltd.
Nippon Life Insurance Company of Japan
Nomura Securities Co., Ltd.
Payden & Rygel
Provident National Bank
Frank K. Reilly, CFA
Salomon Brothers
Sassoon Holdings Pte. Ltd.
Scudder Stevens & Clark
Security Analysts Association of Japan
Shaw Data Securities, Inc.
Sit Investment Associates, Inc.
Standish, Ayer & Wood, Inc.
State Farm Insurance Companies
Sumitomo Life America, Inc.
T. Rowe Price Associates, Inc.
Templeton Investment Counsel Inc.
Travelers Insurance Co.
USF&G Companies
Yamaichi Securities Co., Ltd.

Senior Research Fellows

Financial Services Analyst Association

For more on upcoming Research Foundation publications and webcasts, please visit www.cfainstitute.org/about/foundation/.

Research Foundation monographs are online at www.cfapubs.org.

Made in the USA
Monee, IL
04 November 2026

67376411R00046